PRAISE FOR

WHAT IF YOU TRIED THIS AT WORK?

"*What If You Tried This at Work?* is an invaluable resource that I could immediately apply as an early-stage entrepreneur, especially when success hinges on selecting and managing the right founding team. The book's thirty-six practical vignettes offer clear, cross-functional insights that sharpen managerial skills and inspire actionable strategies. It's a powerful tool for assembling a formidable team and leading with impact right from the start."

—Kelly Barnett, founder and CEO of SoloSpouse

"*What If You Tried This at Work?* sounds the alarm, urging us to recognize how to cross the line that separates 'the everyday from the extraordinary.' The abbreviation 'RISE' will take on a new meaning as Mark Haskins provides the building blocks and essential advice to convert insight into action. This book offers the fuel to accelerate your journey as a manager and leader for those willing to grab the baton."

—Jeff Shuman, board member and former Chief Human Resources Officer at Quest Diagnostics and L3Harris

"A gem of a book for managers and leaders in organizations of all sizes. Mark Haskins distills his undoubted deep wisdom and experience into a series of thirty-six engaging, stand-alone vignettes divided into four themes, making this book an invaluable and effective field guide. Bringing in real-world examples to illustrate many points, his insightful questions at the end of each vignette challenge the reader to ensure personal reflection is followed up with practical action. Given what we know about the impact managers have on the levels of engagement of the people they lead, the learning and changes you make from reading this book could transform your team's culture and performance."

—Anne Gimson, CEO of Strategic Developments (Int.) Ltd. and Editor-in-Chief of *Development & Learning in Organizations*

"*What If You Tried This at Work?* is a roadmap for rethinking how to be the best leader and manager you can be. It is a refreshing and interactive take on traditional management books. Whether read alone or with a close group of motivated professionals, it will help you break out of your routine and be a much more thoughtful and intentional leader at work."

—Kelly Gerhardt, former Director of Strategic Planning of a Fortune 500 retailer

"I met Mark Haskins some years ago after we partnered on an executive leadership program at the Darden School of Business. It was there that I saw firsthand his unique ability to take complex business concepts and make them easily understood to enhance a leader's ability to assess content and make decisions. In this latest book, *What If You Tried This at Work?*, Haskins continues to leverage his unique approach in a simple yet powerful 'field guide' that illustrates the valuable relationship between gaining insights from real-life stories and building capability through continuous practice. Mark gives us a cookbook for sustainable improvement that leads to tangible impact for any leader wanting to continuously learn and grow."

—Andrea Bortner, Chief Human Resources Officer of Grocery Outlet

"Mark Haskins has an extraordinary talent for making management principles resonate. As one of his co-teachers, I've witnessed seasoned executives and rising managers have breakthrough moments, grasping his insights on becoming 'invaluable managers' and more impactful, empathetic leaders. *What If You Tried This at Work?* truly lives up to its promise as a 'field guide of possibilities.' Mark's anecdotes are instantly relatable, sparking those crucial 'aha!' moments every leader seeks. His reflection prompts serve as a catalyst, challenging you to apply his advice to elevate your leadership approach immediately. In a business world often dominated by metrics, Mark's emphasis on empathy and human connection is refreshing and essential. He demonstrates that becoming an invaluable manager stems from consistent, thoughtful actions rather than sweeping initiatives."

—Chic Thompson, founder of WAGiLabs (a global *ideas for good* incubator) and author of *What a Great Idea! 2.0: Unlocking Your Creativity in Business and in Life*

"In this insightful guide, seasoned professor and master of the Socratic method Mark Haskins brings his four decades of experience to the forefront, offering managers a powerful tool for self-improvement. Through short, real-world management vignettes, thought-provoking questions, and reflective exercises, this book acts as a personal coach that fits in your back pocket, always within reach, to help you enhance your managerial capabilities. Whether you're facing daily challenges or aiming for long-term growth, he provides the catalysts to enhance your critical thinking, spark innovative ideas, and take actionable steps."

—Mary Margaret Frank, Dean of Kenan-Flagler Business School, The University of North Carolina at Chapel Hill

"A young Mark Haskins and a senior colleague step into a coffee bar. . . . What happens next makes an indelible impression on Mark, one that triggers a career accumulating invaluable management insights, which Mark has now curated to create this wonderful collection of management 'vignettes'—useful to young managers and veteran executives alike. Like good coffee, RISE up and savor each cup."

—James H. Gilmore, author of *The Experience Economy* and *Look: A Practical Guide for Improving Your Observational Skills*

"Just a few sentences in, and I was hooked. I knew *What If You Tried This at Work?* was on track for impact. I was not disappointed. Every time I read another chapter, I got excited thinking about how I would implement the strategy, technique, or tactic in my own organization and life. Mark has consolidated decades of work into one book. Each chapter is like a year of insights. The book helps with setting the right mindset but also provides practical tools that can be immediately implemented. Anyone who reads this book will find numerous ways to improve their team and even their daily interactions. If you consider yourself a lifelong learner, this book is for you."

—William B. Stilley, CEO and founder of Adovate and former CEO and founder of Adial Pharmaceuticals Inc. (a NASDAQ company)

"Dr. Haskins pulls together decades of experience, providing executive education to our business leaders. The thirty-six insightful and powerful vignettes he presents in *What If You Tried This at Work?* Are a must-read for new and aspiring leaders everywhere. In the unique bonus material section at the end of the book, Dr. Haskins brings his two passions of DIY projects and leadership principles together to craft unique analogies, inviting managers to do the same with their avocational interests. I wish I had a guide like this when I started my career."

—Frederick J. Stefany, Principal Civilian Deputy Assistant Secretary of the Navy for Research, Development & Acquisition
(The view expressed does not necessarily represent the views of the Department of the Navy or the United States.)

What If You Tried This At Work?
A Field Guide of Possibilities for Becoming an Invaluable Manager

by Mark E. Haskins, PhD

© Copyright 2024 Mark E. Haskins, PhD

ISBN 979-8-88824-460-9

All rights reserved. No part of this publication may be reproduced, stored in a retrieval system, or transmitted in any form or by any means—electronic, mechanical, photocopy, recording, or any other—except for brief quotations in printed reviews, without the prior written permission of the author.

Published by

3705 Shore Drive
Virginia Beach, VA 23455
800-435-4811
www.koehlerbooks.com

WHAT IF YOU TRIED  AT WORK?

A Field Guide of Possibilities for Becoming an Invaluable Manager

Mark E. Haskins

VIRGINIA BEACH
CAPE CHARLES

This book is dedicated to all the students, colleagues, and managers I have enjoyed interacting with over the years. Their stories have been my "classroom" for learning.

TABLE OF CONTENTS

Chapter 1- Why Not Now? 1

Chapter 2- Ideas for Action: Self-focused 14

    #1 Fast track. Sidetrack. Backtrack. Off track. Best track. 14

    #2 168! 19

    #3 Different management executives fail
        in amazingly similar ways. 24

    #4 Seize the binding benefits of residential
        management development programs. 31

    #5 Locate, legitimate, liberate, and love leverage. 36

    #6 Be a bridge. Connect others.
        Connect functions. Connect processes. 42

    #7 Hope and osmosis. 48

    #8 Have a freedom fund. 53

Chapter 3- Ideas for Action: Diagnostic-Focused 58

    #9 Focus on focus. 58

    #10 Paint the picture. 65

    #11 Learn from "stay interviews." 69

    #12 One bad constituent-facing employee encounter
        can ruin a relationship. 73

    #13 20/80 or 80/20? 78

    #14 Regularly perform an assumptions audit. 83

    #15 Subject your KPIs to a behavioral audit. 89

    #16 Ask hard questions even when receiving
        good financial news. 95

    #17 Resolve and value disagreements. 101

Chapter 4- Halftime. How Are You Doing? 107

Chapter 5- Ideas for Action: Proactive-Focused 114

    #18 See over the horizon. *114*

    #19 Prototype to accelerate the process. *119*

    #20 LBM—Let go. Back off. Move over. *124*

    #21 A little TPM goes a long way. *129*

    #22 Look for opportunities to develop a "better mousetrap." *133*

    #23 New product ideas can emerge from

        anyone, anywhere, at any time. *139*

    #24 "Never too old to be wrong or too young to be right." *147*

    #25 Simple is in. *152*

    #26 Fundamentals matter. Codify yours. *157*

Chapter 6- Ideas for Action: Interpersonal-Focused...........162

    #27 Be alert! There are at least eleven different

        kinds of intelligence. *162*

    #28 Be alert, again! Adults learn in particular ways. *166*

    #29 Look for opportunities to lead your peers. *171*

    #30 Teams usually perform best under pressure

        or with a high calling. *177*

    #31 What can someone bring? The TEA$^{(squared)}$, of course. *182*

    #32 Empowerment requires enablement and encouragement. ... *189*

    #33 Whenever possible, be more relational

        and less transactional. *195*

    #34 Find and show your softer side. *201*

    #35 Consider making care a core strength. *207*

    #36 Play an ACE as often as you can. *212*

Chapter 7- Find Your Virtuous Cycle 218

Bonus Material- DIY Home Improvement Parallels..........223

Acknowledgments 267

Bio..268

Endnotes 269

CHAPTER 1
Why Not Now?

In school you get the lesson first and then the test.
In life you get the test and then the lesson.[1]

—Tom Groneberg,
author and former full-time rancher

HIS WORDS STRUCK like a midnight bolt of lightning, illuminating the unseen and capturing my full attention. A few years into my career, a senior colleague and I were slowly walking to the coffee bar when he casually asked, "How's it going?"

I absentmindedly replied, "Good. Another day, another dollar."

He stopped, looked me square in the eye, and said, "Maybe you're in the wrong line of work at the wrong place if that is how you feel about a career here."

Awwwwkward! Where does the conversation go now? "How about that basketball game last night?" I quipped, picking up our pace to the coffee bar and a hastily planned escape.

As I thought about that exchange for the next several months, I realized that I could master the tasks my employer was asking of me, but there was more to seek in a career that I hoped would span several decades. With just a few words, my colleague was challenging me to think more broadly and to see the opportunities that existed between the expected and the possible. Had my initial goal been to simply put in my time, collect a paycheck, and not screw up? By default, that might have been. But no. I decided that I wanted to contribute to the institution's mission and culture and to be valued for that—to excel rather than just show up and perform. I wanted to see and seize opportunities that would expand my organizational involvement, stretch my professional and personal capabilities, and energize others. My colleague had done me a great favor in alerting me to a desire for more. I needed an attitude adjustment, a shift in mindset, and a change of heart before it was too late.

Here it is almost forty years after that slow walk to the coffee bar. I have never forgotten that exchange and the wake-up call that came with it. During those ensuing years, I have had the privilege of working with a diverse array of colleagues on a host of issues and with scores of successful organizations of all types—big/little, local/global, governmental/corporate, service/manufacturing, and emergent/mature. After observing, knowing, and interacting with thousands of those organizations' managers, along with my many talented colleagues, I believe successful and aspiring managers all share at least two common traits.

First, the best managers want to do a great job for their employer in both their scripted and unscripted roles, and they want to be known and valued for doing so. Second, and more specifically, they want to have a positive impact on the people, processes, and possibilities associated with what they do at work. That impact may be small, or it may be large. It may be episodic, or it may be ongoing. And it makes no difference whether a manager arrived in their current position of influence via their aspirational pursuit or by taking an unforeseen opportunity. It does not matter if they are young or not. Most everybody harbors a deep desire to be seen, to be valued, and to matter. The best managers use those desires to fuel their journeys.

It matters that people want to matter at work. For many managers, the stress and pressure of their responsibilities can take them down an insidious and subconscious path of, at worst, managing their direct reports as "a means to an end" or, at best, taking them for granted. Moreover, for many other managers, there is a point in their career when it is not enough to have simply gotten the budget submitted on time, designed and implemented a new hiring process, or led the company in repeat customer orders. Such deliverables are important, but nobody wants those cited on their tombstone. In my experience, what will be remembered and what is most enriching over the course of a long and successful management career are one's successful collaborations and lasting relationships.

FOR YOU

THIS BOOK IS for aspiring and current organizational managers who are interested in broadening and improving their management quotient, or MQ^2, with an emphasis on people (MQp)—you, your peers, and your direct reports. It is for those who want to stand out in their organizations as . . .

- people-centric,
    - highly respected,
        - much appreciated,
            - relationally focused,
                - frequently sought out,
                    - world-class colleagues and
                        - collaborative managers.

Think of the managers you have most enjoyed and respected. What was it about them that resonated with you? How did they inspire you? Include you? Teach you? Stretch you? Affirm you? Motivate you? How did their management style affect the way you did things—at work and in life? Understanding your management "roots" offers a chance to identify both your strengths and opportunities for growth. In this book, I present ideas to consider as you think about these questions— based on my own experiences and the conversations I have had with countless managers over the years. I also draw from well-documented stories in the public domain.

Consider for a moment that if we are a parent, volunteer coach, or instructor, we often strive to execute those roles by doing what we saw our own parents, coaches, and instructors do well and by not doing what we thought they did not do well. It's the same in organizations. Managers embrace the approaches that worked for their own role models, casting off the less successful tactics. Along the way, they add their own observations—what worked and what didn't. In essence, they write and revise a management playbook so that over time, those initially formulated dos and don'ts fashion an array of accumulated experiences, hard-earned perspectives, and the continued observation of, and learning from, others.

Are there best practices in organizations? Yes. But the discussion here is about how people express themselves and flourish within those best practices. What do they bring to the table—or Zoom call—that elevates them to their best self and galvanizes others to be the best managers they can be? There are almost as many ways to effectively supervise, lead, and manage as there are people serving in those roles. Consider this: According to the US Bureau of Labor Statistics, there are almost nine million employees in management occupations, and that number is forecasted to grow at 8 percent through 2031.[3] I guarantee that even if you handed the identical "playbook" to all of them, their management style would be their own.

Each successful manager has their own personality, stories, contexts, and areas of expertise that combine to create their own unique way of managing. Even so, there are some common denominators across the successful managers I have had the privilege to meet and work with over the past forty years. And these are the stories I want to tell you. As you read, memories of recent and even long-ago experiences may come to mind—instances in which your managers led, inspired, taught, stretched, or affirmed you and instances in which they fell short, instilling a determination in you to do things differently. This book offers opportunities for reflection on the past and present and the opportunity to fortify or add to your MQ*p* through the discussion of the people-oriented tendencies and attributes I've observed in the successful and valued managers I draw from in these pages.

ABOUT THIS BOOK

WE HAVE ALL read or seen daily devotionals and gratitude journals or perhaps availed ourselves of calendars with daily inspirational messages. We do so to become more focused, to learn, or to recalibrate priorities. These are not how-tos. There are no quizzes. If there are questions, there is no single answer. They exist for reflection. They exist to spark ideas. If reflection leads to ideas, which then leads to action, that's exactly the purpose.

Must that practice be limited to personal exploration? Could managers benefit from similar, regular prompts? Yes. Perhaps daily or weekly entries centered on a short management reading with one or two objectives can help expand the realm of things they do or improve an approach to existing priorities, people, processes, or problems—in essence, raise their MQ*p*.

And that's how this book was conceived. This book presents thirty-six managerial vignettes that managers of all ranks, in all types of organizations, and in almost any locale can embrace to expand and enhance their managerial capabilities. Those vignettes are intended to galvanize and crystallize your reflective thinking and proactive ideas for action. They are straightforward, fundamental, and important. Some may seem ordinary, obvious, and simple. For me, that merely testifies to their relevance and the merit in revisiting them and not overlooking the implications they harbor. Because managers often must work cross-functionally, the book is not just a marketing book, finance book, or any other single-function book. The information presented is drawn from many aspects of the organizational landscape, all germane to the pursuit of a deepened and broadened set of people-focused managerial skills.

The thirty-six entries are grouped into four clusters. Each cluster represents a general, people-oriented focus, with varied entries providing a specific dive into that general theme. The clusters are not mutually exclusive, and some of the content in one cluster is reinforced by that in another. The first cluster primarily focuses on *self*. Where do you find yourself in your managerial journey? How are you doing with some fundamental elements of management? Eight vignettes are posed in this cluster. They are intended to help you establish some important foundational insights about yourself that will be valid throughout your MQp journey. The next nine vignettes are clustered under a *diagnostic*-focused theme. Entries here offer opportunities for periodically assessing the important implications of where your attention is directed and what your presumptive mindset is. The third cluster presents another nine vignettes that encourage you to be *proactive* along some high value-added MQp dimensions. Here, the invitation is to embrace some important foci for action. And finally, the fourth cluster's issues specifically revolve around *interpersonal* opportunities. This final cluster also circles back, in part, to self-awareness themes most conducive to an enhanced interpersonal orientation.

The book is intended to operate as a daily, weekly, or biweekly personal development field journal. As such, each of the book's thirty-six entries begins with a short business insight caption, foreshadowing the theme of the vignette to follow and providing an easily remembered tagline. This caption is followed by a stand-alone vignette presenting a concise, clear managerial insight. At the end of each vignette, there is a set of questions, with blank space after each to capture reactions and thoughts intended to facilitate your progression to planned steps for taking applicable action(s). Sometimes those questions are simply of the "why?" or "why not"? type. Please don't rush past those. Take the time for the introspection they point to. All the questions at the end of each vignette are organized around a **RISE** learning/doing framework. This part of each vignette's entry is important because it invites, funnels, and encourages readers to take action. Reading about something might be interesting, but deep learning is accomplished from action. Collectively, the thirty-six vignettes create a rich mosaic of reality-based, people-focused, useful management insights to spark personal action.

The **RISE** acronym is helpful and hopefully provocative. It denotes four important phases in converting insight to action that will help you to rise up, to rise above, and to become the best manager you can be. You will first be asked to **R**eflect on specific aspects of the vignette you have just read to identify an embedded core principle or practice that most captivates your attention and interest. Such a call encourages you to recollect conversations, observations, experiences, or perceptions from your past to provide some color and emotion to the focus of your reflection. Next, you will be asked a question or two that guides you to **I**dentify a set of realistic opportunities within your current organizational setting for applying the principle or practice just highlighted during your reflection on the reading. Then, you will be prompted, in specific ways, to select an opportunity for action and to **S**hare it with someone to validate its efficacy and fine-tune it. The invitation to share your idea for action builds relational connections, fosters opportunistic collaboration, and heightens a commitment to next steps. The final **RISE** prompt is intended to spur you to act on the focal opportunity previously shared and to then **E**valuate the results of that action for purposes of thinking about how it went, identifying what could have been done better, and how best to continue with it.

Some of the vignettes and related prompts might only pepper a day or two of your time, depending on your interest and desire to dive deep into the topic posed. Others might realistically occupy time and attention for a week or more to address fully. The investment of time for benefitting from this book is up to you. Also, as you will see, the **Share** part usually involves a trusted colleague or friend. It is worth considering using the same person throughout your use of this book, in effect partnering with that person on your MQp development trek.

If that is your inclination, it is important to explain to that person the management development journey you are embarking on and how you would value their participation by being a sounding board for your ideas and an encourager of your pursuits.

The book is not intended to replace a manager's in-depth professional development. It is, however, intended to expand a manager's capabilities and entice them to pursue, with more focused intentionality, those arenas that surface as most interesting or desirous of improvement. To otherwise obtain the crisp insights presented in this book would probably require reading numerous other management books, attending an array of seminars, and obtaining more years of varied managerial experiences. This book can accelerate your MQ*p* development.

OTHER WAYS TO USE THIS BOOK

AT ITS CORE, this is a book best read, embraced, and used at a pace, place, and time of your choosing—one that is comfortable and conducive to focus and taking some preliminary actions. This book's MQ*p* developmental possibilities are, however, not pace-, place-, sequence-, or time- dependent or -constrained. They are open-ended. Each can occupy as much time and energy as you want to devote to it. The vignettes can be selected in any order in accordance with a targeted arena for growth, or they can be selected simply to pursue intriguing developmental paths. Some may appropriately be set aside until a later date, while others are best pursued now.

The **RISE** questions at the end of each vignette are an important part of the learning, and I encourage you to devote time to answering them. We all have our favorite ways to write. The book includes some space for writing. But I recommend giving yourself more room if you can—a notebook or journal if you like to write by hand. If you prefer, open a file on your laptop and type your answers there, or use the dictation function and capture your notes that way. It's for your eyes only, in almost every case. How you participate is up to you.

If you are a mentor to a new manager or someone aspiring to become one, this book can provide topics and foci for scheduled meetings with a protégé. Consider sharing an experience of your own pertaining to the vignette selected for the meeting. In addition to the **RISE** prompts, you could also ask a protégé what they did or didn't like about the managerial insight presented and why. Their responses provide further springboards for discussion that you can pursue.

This book is also suitable for professional development seminars. Instructors can choose which vignettes best align with their instructional objectives. The selections can be assigned and discussed in the seminar or assigned to small groups for report-outs to the larger body.

Young, aspiring managers without a mentor can use this book as a managerial watch list. The vignettes will alert and sensitize the reader to an array of subtle, and perhaps not-so-subtle, managerial capabilities to be on the lookout for in the managers they work with and observe. Seeing an idea in action in one's own circumstance can be a powerful, live case study of a key management principle or practice. And they will no doubt recognize some of the managerial qualities as part of their own behavior, whether learned or instinctual.

Seasoned managers will find the book useful too—whether as a refresher or a source for new concepts and perspectives. Reading and rereading the vignettes can prompt recall of practices or priorities once valued but perhaps now overlooked or undervalued. Bringing pertinent content back to the fore of one's memory and repertoire can be especially important when taking on new or additional managerial responsibilities.

For aspiring or seasoned managers, this book is not really a "one-and-done" read. Both the vignettes provided and the notes you record can provide future reminders and prompts for managerial renewal. That way, it can be a part of your lifelong MQp development, offering the chance to apply questions and ideas sparked by each vignette to new settings, challenges, and possibilities.

Heads up—the book also contains an integration of interests in life that can be mutually beneficial. An insight in one part of life can often spark a parallel insight in another part. Such connections can be reinforcing, elucidating, and sometimes just plain enjoyable. The **bonus material** presented at the book's end is an example of some of those connections for me—organizational management and do-it-yourself (DIY) home improvement projects. They are numbered and titled to correspond to the management entries preceding them. So, the bonus material can be enjoyed in tandem with each management entry in the book or perused after completing the main managerial part of the book.

I am not an expert in DIY, but I have consistently done those sorts of activities my entire adult life. The Tim "the Toolman" Taylor character from the hit syndicated TV series *Home Improvement* might be a somewhat fitting mental image of my DIY endeavors. Nonetheless, through successes and failures, I share DIY stories that have prompted an awareness of a particular management counterpart. Do those stories lead to a deeper understanding of the organizational management insights provided here? Sometimes, yes. They do, however, lead me to a longer-lasting affinity for and remembrance of the insights gleaned, and they do fuel curiosity in search of other parallels that are always enjoyable and energizing. Perhaps these DIY stories will prompt you to find links between your vocational and avocational pursuits. Once you start looking for connections, they just keep surfacing. It is as if your eyes and mind are tuned to a certain frequency, and the same attention-directing voice, whispering similar messages, springs from two different fields, generating memorable and useful insights in stereo. It's fun. It's helpful. It's affirming. The prelude to the bonus material invites you to consider making a similar connecting search. For you, too, it can be fun . . . helpful . . . and affirming.

KEY PREMISES

THE BUILDING BLOCKS of successful and respected management stand on a strong foundation. Likewise, the insights presented in this book rest on several foundational premises. First, do not be fooled—the simplicity of a vignette's insight does not necessarily equate to the easy execution of an emergent idea. Please be intentional, conscientious, and diligent.

Second, the oft-made distinction between management and leadership is not important for the journey posed by this book. I believe management and leadership each involve substantial aspects of the other, either by organizational design, workplace need and opportunity, and/or individual personality. Yes, you may have to "manage" a budget, but that will, of necessity, almost always involve others, directly or indirectly, in coordinating your piece of the organization with theirs. If your management responsibilities involve the work of at least one other person, you can be a leader. In the end, I agree with the former chairman of Intuit: "Your title makes you a manager; your people will decide if you're a leader."[4] This book is intended to help you become the manager that your direct reports and colleagues most want to emulate.

Third, it is important to explicitly state that any actions sparked by the insights gleaned from this book are best undertaken with an authenticity that is genuine and ongoing. Others will readily sense whether your new ways are insincere, one-and-done, or the product of a must-do organizational mandate rather than an I-want-to-earnestly-try-this desire. Complementing an outward authenticity is the internal commitment to an attitude that is mindful of "I want to stick with this until I get better at it." Over time, such an inward attitude will manifest itself outwardly, and others will appreciate the developmental effort you are making.

Fourth, the insights are not directed toward or fueled by a primary objective of maximizing ownership value. If such an outcome results from an organization's managers managing more effectively, insightfully, relationally, and creatively across a spectrum of stakeholders because of the insights teed up here, so be it. The primary objective of this book is the latter, not the former.

Last, almost all things are best when done in concert with at least one colleague or confidant. The final foundational premise undergirding this book is that there are no "lone rangers" here. Input from others along one's MQ*p* development path is invaluable. Colleagues and confidants can constructively act as sounding boards, play devil's advocate, and help in thinking through possibilities, unintended consequences, and helpful connections to make. In many ways, this book is an opportunity for relational management development, not transactional—a theme of vignette #33. Indeed, partnering with a trusted and helpful colleague along the way is a vital step toward a greater emphasis on relational management development.

WHY NOT NOW?

IN A LATE 1789 letter to George Washington, Thomas Jefferson wrote, "The ground I have already passed over enables me to see my way into that which is before me."[5] Indeed, the ground that managers have already explored, stumbled upon, lost their way through, and successfully traversed is full of stories, ideas, and lessons that can benefit not only their continued managerial journey but also that of those who are on their own managerial journey or soon will be. This book shares some of those hard-earned insights from seasoned managers. Of course, it is not comprehensive or authoritative—it does, however, present straightforward, authentic, doable, often overlooked, and undervalued aspects of becoming a more effective person who can both manage and lead. The field-journal nature of this book will help guide you to conscientiously embrace any of the insights that capture your interest because of the reflections asked of you. Mark Greaney, the best-selling author of the *Gray Man* novels, opens one of his books with a quote from Choi Hong Hi[6], founder of the taekwondo martial arts: "Pain is the best instructor, but no one wants to go to his class." To that, I would add that disappointment, failure, and sustainable success are also effective instructors. This book affords you the opportunity to potentially skip the pain, disappointments, and failures classes and go right to the sustainable success classes. Now is as good a time as there will ever be to sign on because "the present is a freely given canvas"[7] on which to craft the managerial life you want to be intentional about having.

CHAPTER 2
Ideas for Action: Self-focused
[vignettes #1–#8]

> **#1 *Fast track. Sidetrack. Backtrack. Off track. Best track.***

I climb, I backtrack. I float. I ramble my way home.[8]

—Mary Oliver,
winner of the Pulitzer Prize for Poetry

HOW FAST, HOW far, how soon? Implicit in the thinking of many talented young managers are tentative answers to such questions. The answers are manifested in different ways: "I'd like to be a North American product manager in five years, with global responsibilities in eight. And I have my eye on the role of executive vice president of marketing for the company in twelve." Such aspirational thoughts can be energizing and motivating. Clearly, a prerequisite for getting on the fast-track managerial train is excelling at what you have been assigned to do. After that, the fast track can often unfurl by becoming known for speaking candidly, insightfully, and considerately in meetings. Invitations to take on special assignments are likely to arise, along with opportunities to volunteer for high-profile, challenging tasks. Then, delivering on-time, on-budget, collaborative results gets noticed and appreciated. Exhibiting an interest in and an ability to work cross-functionally with patience, inclusiveness, and graciousness will also get an aspiring young manager noticed. In just the past handful of years, I know of several colleagues for whom such contexts and capabilities catapulted them into new, major managerial roles.

There are also sidetrack possibilities along the way. It often starts with fast-track potential and opportunities but ends, at least for a season, if not permanently, with the manager being sidelined. Being sidelined means that a person, by organizational choice, reverts to just the primary role and responsibilities that they most recently held or that they were originally hired to do. That person is still a full player but is no longer in the high-potential cohort for a senior-level manager or executive consideration. One's boss is not likely to ever convey such news, but sidetracks provide front-row seats to see the fast trackers go by. I know. I've experienced the displacement from the fast track to the sidetrack. A quick way to end up on the sidetrack is to say no to the opportunities offered. Guilty. Top management will only ask a couple of times. Another switch that sends someone over to the sidetrack, off the fast track, is to acquire the reputation for being impatient, brash, ungrateful, or all of these. Guilty again.

And then, there is the young professional who fails at the managerial opportunities they have been given. Failure can obviously be due to a lack of capability and/or ethical behavior. I have seen both. In my experience, what also appears as an underlying root cause for a career that goes off track or even backtracks is due to unwanted and unwarranted speech. Clearly, bigoted remarks are out of bounds. So too, however, are remarks that are disrespectful, condescending, needlessly confrontational, and dismissive. Yes, it is true that a picture is worth a thousand words, as the saying goes, and yet it only takes a few wrong words to derail a career. A backtracked managerial career is one that either comes to an end or becomes so constrained that it is uninspiring, mostly rote, and void of fulfillment.

The best managerial track is specific to the individual. For me, the hallmarks of that are:

- it provides opportunities for important organizational contributions,
- it involves others, and
- it presents the right pace and alignment with my capabilities and talents and provides episodic opportunities for stretching into new arenas.

If I find myself stressed, with sleepless nights, or foregoing family time, those are the quiet signals that my "track" is too fast. On the other hand, if I am bored, easily distracted, or frequently critical of my employer or colleagues, those are signals that I need to step up and step out and strive to make a positive difference by taking on something more and/or new.

REFLECT: *Are you doing what you want to be doing and where you want to be doing it? Is it fulfilling, and if so, in what way(s)? Be as specific as you can be. Are those fulfillment factors likely to be ongoing or not? If not, what would it take to make them so? If you are not doing what you want to be doing, where you want to be doing it, why not? Are those reasons under your control or others'? Are they changeable or not? Overall, and in hindsight, have you accepted and declined the opportunities that have come your way with the wisdom and clarity of purpose that you wish you had brought to bear on those opportunities? If not, why not? Do you believe you are on track, off track, or backtracking in your career? If you believe you are not on track (be ruthlessly honest with yourself), why not?*

_____

_____

_____

IDENTIFY: *What one or two specific aspects of your current job can you effectively offload so that you are in a better position to take on a new, intriguing, enriching responsibility? Where would you anticipate that new responsibility would lead you? Is that really where you want to go, and why? Revisit your specific career aspirations. Do they need to be revised, reinforced, or replaced? What one or two steps can be taken in that regard? Perhaps your priorities have changed, and/or you have learned of new paths and opportunities to pursue that you had not seen before. If so, detail that new direction, identifying the necessary steps to embark on it.*

SHARE: *With one or two specific career ideas in mind, take two steps. First, is there a safe role model for such a direction and path to whom you can talk about your ideas? If so, be proactive in meeting with that person. Second, is there a close friend and confidant that you can "test" your thinking with to get their helpful reaction(s)? If so, find a comfortable time to do so. In both instances, be as concrete as possible as to what you see as needed for progression toward your desired career destination. In doing so, it is important to be realistic about timing and capabilities. Ask your confidant if they believe you have what it takes to accomplish what you are mapping out. It is worthwhile to explore and discuss your underlying motives and* *the destination you are articulating. Do they sound energizing and sustainable to your confidant?*

_____
_____
_____
_____

EVALUATE: *After sharing your thoughts with another person or two and getting their input, craft a career plan document. Be as specific as you can be. Set it aside for a couple of weeks and revisit it to see if it still resonates and energizes you. If it does, schedule a meeting with your boss to go over it and to see what their reaction to it is and the extent to which they will help you develop along those lines. Be conscious of not just what you are asking for from your employer but also what things you can do for the organization for it to be exciting and encouraging. What developmental arenas do you need to address? What deliverables do you need to succeed in providing? What colleagues should you partner with and learn from along the way? Finalize your career plan document after that meeting and refer to it regularly to consider where you are on your timeline and whether it is still a match for your aspirations.*

_____
_____
_____
_____

...ANOTHER CHAPTER 2 VIGNETTE...

> *#2 168!*

61.11 × 52 × 168 = 533,857 average adult lifetime hours[9]

AN ADULT CAN impact the world with 533,857 available hours. Indeed, a valued long-time colleague, Jim Clawson, devoted much of his career to encouraging and helping managers be more conscientiously purposeful with their time, talents, and energy. It was his observation that much of what managers do is fueled by inertia, familiarity, or custom and thus becomes habit. In that context, he challenged managers with two simple foci: the number 168 and the word *choice*. There are 168 hours in a week. And our days are filled with many choices, subconscious and conscious ones. These two foci are provocative when connected. Indeed, we all have the choice of how to allocate our 168 hours across a spectrum of needs and wants, dos and don'ts, musts and likes. Preferably, those choices result in positive, sustainable, and energized engagement with others and with tasks.

I want to get seven hours of sleep each night, devote about two hours each day to meals, and spend no more than one hour each day traveling to and from the various places I must go (e.g., work, errands, kids, etc.). Thus, 70 of my 168 weekly hours are quickly spoken for and used up. What do I do with the other 98? On average, about 50 of those hours are devoted to work-related activities for my employer.

Two points then arise. First, how do I typically spend those 50 work-related hours? Recently, approximately 10 of those hours have been devoted to my student classroom obligations. Another 5 hours are spent in meetings or are devoted to pre- or post-meeting tasks. On average, 5 more hours a week are focused on professional consulting-type activities. If I am honest, another 5 hours per week are spent socializing/interacting with colleagues in the hallways, in their offices, around the coffee machines, and before/after meetings. Thus, the remaining 25 work-related hours each week are available for research and writing. That seems about right for my goals and energy.

Second, what happens to the remaining, nonwork-related 48 hours? To be honest, I am a bit surprised to find that I have so many discretionary hours available. I thought I was extremely busy. Are my choices pertaining to those hours purposefully considered, or do they disappear because of habitual routines and mindless busyness? Am I pleased with how those hours get used? I am not sure I am going to like the answers to such questions.

> **REFLECT:** *Determine, on average, the available hours you have each week for work and personal time after accounting for sleep, eating, and necessary travel. Of those available hours, how many pertain to work? Partition those work-related hours into meaningful groups that might include foci like core/required tasks, meetings (internal versus external), problem-solving, opportunity seeking, customer/client interactions, colleague interaction, learning, data analysis, mentoring, and new business development. Use groupings that are distinctive and most pertinent to you. Next, of the overall weekly available hours initially identified, subtract the total work-related hours. That resulting number pertains to your weekly discretionary time. On average, label as best as you can how those hours get used.*
>
> *Helpful questions to also consider as you reflect: How many hours a week are devoted to work? Do I make the effort to spend*

a little time each day with a colleague or two discussing not just business but meaningful personal matters—getting to know that person a little better? How much time each day do I invest in my own learning or that of a close colleague or a direct report? Do I often/seldom try something new or outside my comfort zone? Do I tend to opt out of opportunistic conversations, or do I seize those moments for sharing, explaining, discussing, debating, exploring ideas, and establishing relationships? Am I on the lookout for opportunities to affirm and thank someone? If not, why not? If not, who might be a prime candidate for me to do that with? Similar questions can be posed for your nonwork hours. Am I energized by how I have been allocating my time? Why or why not?

_____

_____

_____

_____

IDENTIFY: *For your work-related hours, review the hours associated with each grouping you established. Compare those numbers with what you would like to see. Isolate the one or two functions or activities with the biggest differential between actual versus desired hours. Consider what you might be able to do to shrink those differentials—spending less time on the things that seem to occupy too much time and devoting more time to those things that you are under-investing time in. Perhaps there are some things you would like to be doing that currently receive none of, or very little of, your time—what are those things, and what can you do about them? Repeat this process for your nonwork-related hours. What must you change, if anything, to have more energy and joy flow from the work and personal time allocations you make?*

_____
_____
_____
_____

SHARE: *Approach a conscientious colleague with your idea(s) for how you want to try to shrink the significant time differentials you identified earlier. Ask for their reactions to your idea(s) and if they have any pertinent ideas for you drawn from their own experience of a similar situation. For the nonwork-related time differential idea(s) you crafted, ask a spouse, partner, or good friend for their reactions and inputs. For both the work-related and nonwork-related ideas that you decide to implement, consider asking your sounding-board person if they would help/join/assist you in your endeavor.*

_____
_____
_____
_____

EVALUATE: *After a month or two, how did your efforts to redeploy your hours go? What got in the way? And what might you be able to do about that? What facilitated your redeployment, and what might you be able to do to nurture/perpetuate that facilitative context or assistance? Do you feel more in control of, or more purposeful in, how your time is spent than you did before? More energized? More joyful? Why or why not? Habits are hard to break. Are there some that have surfaced that you must be mindful of and purposeful in breaking, and if* *so, what and how? Are there other people you can reach out to for further assistance in becoming more conscientious about how you spend your time and in mitigating the habits that hinder that pursuit? If so, challenge one another along those lines for the benefit of both of you.*

_____
_____
_____
_____
_____

... ANOTHER CHAPTER 2 VIGNETTE...

> **#3 *Different management executives fail in amazingly similar ways.***

*... there's no success like failure.
And that failure's no success at all.*[10]

—Bob Dylan,
singer/songwriter with multiple Grammy awards

AS I INTERACT with hundreds of successful organizational managers every year, I am convinced there is no single best way to manage or lead. Not only does the personality of an individual influence their personal managerial approach, but so do the constituency contexts they face, the resources available, the challenges encountered, and all prior experiences. At the most fundamental level, a manager's task is to successfully navigate their project, team, division, or organization from here to there—like GPS. A simple task, but as it is with the GPS information we can access in our cars, there is often more than one way to get from here to there. There are, however, some routes to avoid—just as in the management realm, where there are means and paths to be avoided. In thinking about the managerial routes to avoid—those metaphorical traffic jams, detours, potholes, and work zones—I keep returning to author Sydney Finklestein's *Why Smart Executives Fail*. He identifies "seven habits that characterize spectacularly unsuccessful [managers and executives]." Many, he writes, "exhibit all seven."[11] I note several below for your consideration from the same book.

"They see themselves and their companies as dominating their environments" (p. 214).

I can remember Trans World Airlines Inc., Braniff International Airways, and Pan American World Airways, Inc. as premier international airlines. They are now gone. New operating models and financial structures gave rise to successful newcomers—companies like Southwest Airlines Company, JetBlue Airways Corp., and Spirit Airlines Inc.—displacing some of those thought to be unbeatable. In various ways, the same is true for once-dominant or popular companies like Burger Chef fast-food restaurants, A&P grocery stores, and Compaq portable computers. I remember each of these. I was a customer. They are all gone. What organization is next? Chances are that its managers will have thought it impossible due to their historical prominence. And the public may not even notice their displacement and quiet disappearance.

"They think they have all the answers" (p. 223).

It is always important for a manager to know what they don't know. Thinking that you have the most valuable insights points to an untruth and is a prime indicator of an inability or unwillingness to listen to others or invest in personal preparation and learning. It is clear evidence of hubris that is off-putting to others and preemptive of potentially useful dissent. It can needlessly lead to suboptimal performance/outcomes. I learned this the hard way. As a young professional, I was invited, with much flattery, to give a presentation at a conference. I thought I must have the valuable insights most wanted/needed by those attending. I didn't. It was an embarrassing experience and a profoundly missed opportunity.

"They ruthlessly eliminate anyone who isn't 100 percent behind them" (p. 226).

Alfred Sloan, an early, successful chairman of the board at General Motors Company, is reported to have said in a meeting where everyone seemed too quickly, easily, and unanimously to arrive at agreement on a decision-making challenge, "Gentlemen, I take it we are all in agreement on the decision here . . . [therefore] I propose we postpone further discussion of this matter until our next meeting to give ourselves time to develop disagreement and perhaps gain some understanding of what the decision is all about."[12] Such an attitude is just the opposite of eliminating dissenters—it is valuing them, wanting them. When such voices are raised in a respectful, informed manner, dissenters are helpful, not harmful.

"They underestimate major obstacles" (p. 231).

Managers can be prone to underestimating the resources (time, talent, money) needed to comply with new regulations, enter new geographic markets, find, hire, and retain the best people, upgrade facilities and services, and overcome unfavorable public relations. A "can-do" attitude fosters confidence but can also contribute to unrealistic estimates of effort and time needed to address a problem or seize an opportunity. Moreover, when addressing obstacles and problems, managers sometimes fail to vet proposed solutions for unintended consequences as thoroughly as they should. Thus, taking one action (e.g., cutting salespeople commission plans) to address one problem (e.g., high overhead costs) may simply lead to another problem (e.g., reduced morale amongst the sales force) or to a compounding of the initial one (e.g., reduced value-added customer interactions by salespeople, leading to reduced sales)—this is, in part, the story of Circuit City, a once prominent electronics retailer.[13]

"They stubbornly rely on what worked for them in the past" (p. 235).

In the early twenty-first century, one of the United States' largest general merchandise retailers, Kmart, declared bankruptcy and reorganized. Shortly thereafter, Kmart purchased Sears, Roebuck and Co., another large iconic US general merchandise retailer that was experiencing some of its own financial struggles. Not quite fifteen years after that merger, the newly combined company declared bankruptcy.

Consider for a moment this related point. A dear mentor of mine used to preach the merits of "bulldog tenacity" when things are not unfolding according to your hopes or plans. This is often thought of as grit or perseverance—worthy attitudes to bring to bear to get through tough times. But admirable grit and perseverance adapts, adjusts, and considers alternative ways of accomplishing a desired objective. To some extent, it is true that, as the popular saying goes, "Insanity is doing the same thing over and over and expecting a different outcome." For some observers, it was never quite clear how the merger of a struggling Kmart with a struggling Sears was ever going to result in a successfully combined organization. In the end, it didn't.

Too much talk, too little action.

This is a shortcoming that I want to add to the list for consideration. Meetings, task forces, ad hoc study groups, white papers, best practices research, focus groups, and all such endeavors that foster discussion and debate can each have a purposeful place in the life of an organization. Such venues and undertakings, however, do reach a point of diminishing returns. Stop. Will one more meeting, one more line of inquiry, or one more comparative study make a difference? More talk may feel like progress or further evidence of due diligence pursued, but it may not be. Make some initial decisions. Make some trial moves. Like letting the air out of a balloon, too much talk can deflate built-up energy and enthusiasm for a potentially positive course of action. Too much talk can delay actions that then handicap competitive positions. Too much talk may prevent insights better learned via actions taken and results assessed. Too much talk may signal too much caution, too much risk aversion.

There are lessons to be learned from all such managerial failures. Let's acknowledge them. Let's avoid them.

REFLECT: *How do you define career success? Are there multiple dimensions to that definition? If so, what are they, and* *how would you rank them in importance? What will success create for you, and what is the relative importance of those outcomes? On what dimensions of success, as you have envisioned it, have you not yet succeeded? Is it just a matter of time before you will, or have you failed in some way in that pursuit? If you have, why? Do you see in yourself any of the managerial shortcomings noted above? Which? Are there other reasons for failing along some important career dimension(s), and if so, what are they? As you answer these questions, try not to externalize the reasons—focus on what you have and have not done and why.*

_____
_____
_____
_____

IDENTIFY: *What do you need to do better or differently to be more firmly on the path of success as you desire it? Do you need to modify your definition of success, and if so, in what way? For any failure you identified earlier, can that shortcoming be addressed, and if so, in what way? What two or three steps can you take now to embark on a path to address the root cause of a failure and/or the aftermath of a failure?*

Note: We have all failed at work in some way—mostly small failures, setbacks, disappointments, but failures of some sort, nonetheless. If you are inclined to dismiss, discount, or deny any failure, why is that? Are you as aware and as honest as you can be in seeing shortcomings? If not, why not?

_____
_____
_____

SHARE: *In a quiet place, without distractions, share and compare your definition of success with that of a trusted peer. Given your definition, ask that person if they see you as successful or on the way to becoming successful. Share with them your assessment, noting any shortcomings (like those presented above or others) that you perceive to be true for yourself. Then, share with them the two or three steps you identified to address that shortcoming. Ask for their input regarding the feasibility, appropriateness, and robustness of your planned steps. Listen for ways they might be helpful to you, and do not hesitate to ask for their assistance, even if it is merely to check in occasionally.*

EVALUATE: *How did it go? Was the conversation with your peer fruitful or uncomfortable? If it was uncomfortable, why? Might the reasons for that discomfort also point to an area for personal development, and if so, in what way? Have you been successful in addressing, to some extent, any underlying reasons for having previously failed? And if so, note those reasons and feel good about having accomplished that. If not, why not? Going forward, what will it take to stay on topic, be vigilant, and be purposeful to mitigate or eliminate those previously identified shortcomings or reasons for failure? Through this process, have you felt the desire to modify or expand your definition of success,* *and if so, in what way(s)? Does your definition of success involve others in ways that are more likely than not to lead to their success too? If not—take a pause here to get clear on this—why not?*

_____
_____
_____
_____
_____

...ANOTHER CHAPTER 2 VIGNETTE...

> **#4 *Seize the binding benefits of residential management development programs.***

[Meriwether Lewis] wanted to know the why as well as the way of things.[14]

—STEPHEN AMBROSE,
author and renowned military historian

OVER THE YEARS, I have worked with several organizations that wanted my colleagues and me to design and deliver customized management development programs for them. The major themes they wanted those programs to address ran the gamut from general business acumen to high-performing partnerships to strategic decision-making and other topics of a similar ilk. Even though different organizations sought different program themes, there was a common denominator amongst the organizations' requests: the perception that their organizations were not as internally coordinated/connected and strategically attuned as they wanted them to be. Why not? They attributed this lack of cohesion to several factors: ever-increasing geographical dispersion of their organizational units, a high percentage of existing managers having come from numerous outside entities, and the recent retirement of many long-serving managers with a vast amount of institutional knowledge and familiarity.

Yes, the current management group had the same company name on their paychecks, and they even nominally shared the same core operating practices and some of the same approaches to sales and service, quality control, and performance reviews. Yet the top management teams that contacted us believed that many organizational boundaries needed to be spanned and broadened personal relationships established. In their thinking, online and virtual management development initiatives were not sufficient and were no substitute for face-to-face residential investments in management development. Indeed, as Warren Buffett has noted, "You're more likely to be on the same page when you're in the same room."[15] There were functional, geographic, cultural, product/service lines, and senior/junior boundaries that they wanted to dissolve. Moreover, they believed that within their organizations, there was a vast and untapped reservoir of wisdom and best practices that, if accessed and shared across their management personnel, would propel their organizations to better performance. Their managers could not only learn from expert instructors but also from one another. Thus, the management development programs we were to design and deliver would host managers from across all such boundaries to, in part, tap the best of what each program attendee could bring. Those programs benefited from adult learners as the targeted group—people who had the experiences and maturity to know a bit about what they didn't know and who had real-world contexts for applying what they were going to be asked to learn.

The final program designs we delivered provided significant opportunities for personal networking that sanctioned and fostered discussions of a common set of governance and constituent approaches. The programs helped connect the widely dispersed and differentiated managers to meet and work with one another in an off-site, learning-infused environment. The program designs concentrated on seizing and leveraging opportunities for:

- face-to-face relationship building amongst the attendees,
- the creation of intercountry and cross-functional project teams,

- building shared knowledge of best practices and/or new approaches to key organizational endeavors,
- crafting and explaining commitments for a personal management initiative or two,
- strengthening a sense of the organization's culture, history, and values, and
- sanctioning the expression of shared hopes and dreams for one's workplace team, organizational unit, and/or the enterprise overall.

It is that intangible, informal, interpersonal connection, born of face-to-face connections and conversations, that is the glue that binds people to one another, and that, in turn, creates an organization capable of providing seamless, effective service.[16] And, as anyone who has attended an offsite residential management development program knows, a significant challenge exists upon returning to work. The energy, enthusiasm, ideas, and resolutions proclaimed while away can dissipate quickly when back in the normal rhythms of work, facing a pressing array of responsibilities. One of the best ways to combat that is to have managers accept the mantle of teachers upon their return. And so the managers become teachers. Yes, managers manage resources, but managers also instruct, explain, and model for the benefit of the people on their teams.

My colleagues and I encouraged our program attendees to return to their organizations with an agenda of sharing with their teams what they had learned and the possibilities they envisioned for those teams—in essence, to become teachers too! Sharing what they learned keeps it alive for them and invites others to embrace the lessons and even support the managers in their own new outlook. By its very nature, teaching expands the population of learners, who can then also become teachers to others. Such beneficial and cascaded learning best stems from an attitude of intentionality, making sure it happens. "Sharing information creates a shared reality"[17] within and across an organization—a boundary-busting practice worth pursuing.

WHAT IF YOU TRIED THIS AT WORK?

REFLECT: *When was the last time you actively and conscientiously adopted the role of learner in concert with a cadre of colleagues? What were some of the benefits you experienced from that endeavor, and what similar experiences would you be interested in pursuing today? Have you avoided going off site for professional development, and if so, why, and are those reasons valid, or are they excuses? Be honest.*

_____
_____
_____
_____

IDENTIFY: *What would you most like to learn in the coming year that would (a) benefit your organization, (b) contribute to your personal growth, and (c) be best done (or most enjoyably done) in collaboration with others from your organization? Be as specific as you can be. What would it take for that to happen? Who can make that happen? Where and with whom can it happen?*
Identify internal and external thought leaders you would like to learn from and whose expertise could benefit a wider circle of colleagues within your organization. Make the case for offering this type of professional development program. List both intangible and tangible outcomes, such as culture-building and compliance awareness, team-building and talent development, and strategic and operational benefits.

_____
_____
_____
_____

SHARE: *Solicit a handful of colleagues most likely to see the merits of your learning proposal and the case for it. Share with them the perceived need for a professional development program like the one you envision and invite their support. Share with them a brief document you have prepared, making the case for the organizational investment in such an endeavor. With their assistance, fine-tune it with the ultimate intention of presenting it to the organizational decision-maker.*

_____
_____
_____
_____

EVALUATE: *Did your proposal meet with approval, and will an off-site management development initiative take place? If yes, what factors won the day? If not, why not, and are those reasons resolvable? Is there a smaller-scale version of what you sought to do that could be done for your direct reports and by you? In this regard, listen to your own thoughts that surface and signal a "no." The answer can be "yes," and take the time to make the case to yourself. Could you lead or colead a scaled-down version? Teaching is an important managerial capability that involves the holistic task of (a) identifying a learning need, (b) designing an experience to address that need, and (c) finding the right resources for delivering the desired learning to whom it will be most beneficial. You can do it.*

_____
_____
_____
_____

... ANOTHER CHAPTER 2 VIGNETTE ...

> **#5 *Locate, legitimate, liberate, and love leverage.***

When we leverage, we aggregate and organize existing resources to achieve success.[18]

—Richie Norton,
best-selling author and sought-after CEO coach

IN TODAY'S ORGANIZATIONAL vernacular, operating leverage is the capacity and ability to derive greater outputs from a given level of resources. Generating more factory production with no additional factory investment, for example. Or getting greater sales territory coverage with the same sales force. Or expanding a charity's donor list without adding more fundraisers to the payroll. My experience has been that, all too often, managers desire greater leverage, study how to achieve it, utilize technology to capture it, celebrate when improved leverage is achieved, and then fail to push further to fully exploit the opportunity for even a bit more leverage. In essence, this "leaving money on the table" phenomenon is often due to one of two factors: an inability to see beyond the immediate goal (a "satisficing" mindset) or an inability to creatively see the value resident in a leverage 2.0 initiative (a "stuck-in-the-box" mindset).

Breakthrough leverage can usually be achieved through one or more of these five resource considerations:

- fully focused utilization of existing resources,

- less redundant and leaner resources,
- applied creativity with existing resources,
- synergistic, connected uses of resources, and
- high-quality resources from a few highly reliable sources.

1. FULLY FOCUSED UTILIZATION OF EXISTING RESOURCES is a good place to start. A classic example is the original Dell Computer Corp.'s initial, single, steadfast focus on direct end-user distribution without intermediaries. Order taking, production information systems, and shipping information were all centered on interfacing with the end user. There was no need for a vast array of retailers. Locally, there are some other examples. The Market at Grelen uses its 1,000 acres not just to grow and sell trees and flowering plants, as they began doing in the 1990s. They now have sections for customers to pick their own fruits and vegetables. They have cleared and maintained walking trails throughout their property for visitors to use. They have a café and gift shop. They have facilities positioned to capture the beauty of the surrounding countryside for hosting conferences, weddings, and private gatherings. They have seasoned employees who provide expertise across all these functions. Grelen has found ways to fully utilize its picturesque rural setting. Likewise, Afton Mountain Vineyards, in addition to all the normal winery activities, has a handful of modern cabins on the property for rent to overnight guests. And most, if not all, wineries in this region are available for weddings and other large gatherings.

2. LESS REDUNDANT AND LEANER RESOURCES provide another means for improved leverage. Organizations that move toward consolidating once-dispersed functions (e.g., purchasing, HR, accounting, and engineering) are seeking to have less duplication and more streamlined and efficient infrastructures. AES Corporation, headquartered near Washington DC, had such a major thrust across its global operations a few years back. This is often a critical undertaking that is typically sparked by the post-merger integration (PMI) activities of almost any organization that has chosen to grow via mergers and/or partnerships and/or strategic alliances. What do we have two of? Marketing directors? Finance divisions? Where do we go from here? How do we become—and remain—lean?

3. APPLIED CREATIVITY WITH EXISTING RESOURCES. Where I live, a very successful sandwich shop saves all the ends they cut off the baguettes when making delicious sandwiches. Those ends are bagged and sold as an additional product. In the gig economy, we see individuals with existing resources that can bring income: renting a spare bedroom (or their entire home) via Airbnb or driving their personal car for Uber or Lyft. Applying creativity to existing resources need not always result in cutting costs or generating revenue to create value. Empty seats on an organization's private plane are a literal representation of an unused resource. Selling empty seats is not an option. But those organizations can register with the nonprofit Corporate Angel Network, offering available seats on their existing flights to transport cancer patients and family members to distant care destinations free of charge. While not a revenue stream, such a service is a wonderful contribution to communities and a meaningful way to be a good corporate citizen.

4. SYNERGISTIC, TARGETED USES OF RESOURCES can create leverage. Consider the battery-operated power tool market. Makita Corp. and Stanley Black & Decker, Inc. each leverage their own unique battery designs to foster consumers' purchases of their nail guns, drills, hedge shears, string trimmers, and other such common tools from within their own family of products. Within their product line, the batteries are interchangeable. Each suite of tools, however, can only use the battery from its own manufacturer—that is, Makita battery packs do not fit Stanley Black & Decker battery-powered tools and vice versa. Thus, one battery design fuels an ever-expanding array of tools that use it, creating (if not requiring) brand loyalty; customers think twice about the extra cost and inconvenience before bringing in another brand and another battery type. Another great example is YUM! Brands, Inc., which owns thousands of Pizza Hut, Taco Bell,

Habit Burger Grill, and Kentucky Fried Chicken restaurants Their leverage solution is a third-party procurement cooperative to pool that collective purchasing power.

5. HIGH-QUALITY RESOURCES FROM A FEW HIGHLY RELIABLE SOURCES are a final means of achieving sustainable and value-added leverage. Perhaps the popularity of this approach can be attributed to General Motors Company in the 1990s. The company was struggling financially, and a major change came with the appointment of Ignacio Lopez as vice president of worldwide purchasing. He had successfully reduced supplier costs in GM's European operations, and he was brought in to do the same for GM on an even grander scale. His solution was to develop and deploy teams[19] of GM engineers and other experts to the company's network of suppliers to find ways for *them* to become more efficient and thus more cost effective. Those suppliers' efficiencies would then factor into GM's negotiated purchase prices. As you might imagine, issues ultimately arose as to inequities in bargaining power and who most benefited from the improved efficiencies. Nevertheless, the concept of a well-vetted, select supplier list whose members gain more exclusive commitments in exchange for cost savings to the purchaser took root. This strategy is now referred to as strategic sourcing.[20] Apple Inc. and Nestlé are often touted as contemporary models of this approach.[21]

These five resource foci can help spark leverage ideas. In seeking value-creating sustainable leverage, the first thing to do is identify your organization's underutilized resources—people, facilities, expertise, locations, processes, technologies . . . what else? With that list in hand—and it may be a list of one thing or quite a few things—begin imagining the possibilities. Use these five resource considerations as your guide. Be on the lookout for leverage possibilities.

REFLECT: *What organizational resources are under your control and/or available for your use? Start with facilities,* *equipment, and talent. For each specific item you list, note the ways in which your organization utilizes them and benefits from them. With those uses as a given, what else could each of those items you listed contribute—think creatively and unabashedly? Spend some time thinking about the various ways you have seen other organizations creatively expand the utilization of their facilities, equipment, and talent for their internal benefit, for the community, or for additional revenue streams. Next, think intra-organizationally and go prospecting. What facilities, equipment, and talent are located elsewhere within your larger organization that might effectively be brought to bear on a need (or opportunity) where you work and where you have responsibilities?*

_____
_____
_____
_____
_____

IDENTIFY: *Zero in on one or two specific resources that you believe harbor potentially leverageable benefits. What steps are needed to pursue those leverage-induced benefits? Take a shot at sizing the magnitude of the effort to bring about that leverage as well as the nature, timing, and extent of the resulting benefits. Quick, sustainable successes are best to target at the outset—something doable.*

_____
_____
_____
_____
_____

SHARE: *After thinking through the steps needed to pursue a leverage opportunity, who are the best people with whom to discuss feasibility and, ultimately, implementation? Share your idea(s) and invite those folks to:*
- *Highlight additional issues you may not have noted,*
- *Share similar examples elsewhere within or outside the organization,*
- *Help you fine-tune the steps you want to embark on to accomplish the targeted leverage, and*
- *Provide you with further support and assistance.*

_____
_____
_____
_____

EVALUATE: *How did it go? Did the vetting of your idea with others meet with enthusiasm or not? Why? Did the execution of your idea meet with success or not? Why? Did you find it unexpectedly difficult, or relatively easy, to carry out your leverage initiative? Why? Did the intended benefits materialize or not? Why? Is your leverage initiative replicable or not? If yes, what will that require? If not, why not, and is it worthwhile to address those reasons? The desire for leveraged and leverageable resources will remain a fact of organizational life. How can you best inculcate that need into an everyday managerial mindset for yourself and your direct reports?*

_____
_____
_____
_____

... ANOTHER CHAPTER 2 VIGNETTE ...

> **#6 *Be a bridge. Connect others. Connect functions. Connect processes.***

> *... build bridges, not walls.*[22]
>
> —Pope Francis

FUNCTIONAL SILOS CAN be very problematic. When different departments and units are compartmentalized, the entire organization can suffer. Reduced efficiency and redundant efforts cost organizations money. Communication barriers arise and can curtail innovation, hampering collaboration and slowing down problem-solving and decision-making.

Collaborative integration is almost always better. It incorporates diverse perspectives from employees with different backgrounds and areas of expertise, banding together to devise innovations or resolve problems in ways that simply couldn't happen in isolation. When recurring cross-departmental connections occur, strategic and operational cohesion improves, and a culture of learning and creativity can blossom.

Stepping into a model of collaborative networks requires someone of influence to model collaborative integration while actively championing it. The most direct and visible way to model it is by being a bridge builder between distinct and/or disparate parts of the organization. It requires managers to be attuned to and somewhat savvy about the arenas outside their primary sphere of responsibility.

Organizations need managers who can artfully and accurately speak the language of, for example, both accounting and manufacturing, both HR and organizational culture, both business development and client service, both fundraising and organizational mission, both talent development and strategy, or both engineering and marketing. If you realize you lack organizational dual- or tri-fluency, it's not exactly bad news but rather a perfect opportunity to build a bridge, walk across it, and expand your fluencies and connections.

I have known a manager to step away from her corporate flight department role to experience corporate strategy/business development. Another manager moved from his health-care department management role into an organizational information technology role. In another instance, I witnessed a statistics professor seize the opportunity to teach finance. Such individual, simple initiatives provided much personal growth and organizational integration and connections and resulted in cross-functional, cross-departmental perspectives being brought to bear on issues and opportunities. All that was needed was for one individual and their organization to see and seize the merits of an opportunity and an appropriate moment to make a move for connection and integration.

Reaching across silos garners even more momentum and benefit when formal tools or processes are put in place that foster a healthy reliance on those outside our silo. When employees see the bigger picture—learn how what they do and think affects what others do and think—networks integrate, engagement can increase, and innovation has room to flourish.

For example, these benefits are evident in the interrelated areas of product design, manufacturing, and marketing. My former colleague Shahid Ansari coauthored a great book with his wife, Jan Bell, titled *Target Costing: The Next Frontier in Strategic Cost Management*. You can tell by the title that John Grisham has nothing to worry about and that it is not a book intended for bedtime reading. But it's an example of a formal process designed for bridge-building.

It describes a process that companies use to connect engineering, manufacturing, and marketing. The goal is obvious: ascertain which products/services, with which features, and at what price customers want and are willing to pay.

Such alignment is often one of the major tensions and challenges within an organization. According to Ansari and Bell, finding an answer involves using several planning process steps with cross-functional benefits, including:

- the quality functional deployment (QFD) process, which helps determine customers' relative weightings of product/service features,
- value indexing, which identifies which product/service components need cost reductions, which don't, and which can be enhanced,
- employing cost estimation tables to track a product's/service's cost as it goes from concept to final design,
- incorporating value engineering processes that enable informed product/service cost reductions with no loss of product/service functionality, and
- cost tracking tools to monitor progress toward the overall targeted cost.[23]

Designing product features and service delivery elements without tending to these considerations wastes time, energy, and money. Why devote resources to engineering features and elements the customer does not value? This particular process facilitates the strategic investment of operational resources where you can get the best return on investment by prioritizing the features and benefits customers most value. "If you build it, they will come" may work for a fictional baseball story as in the *Field of Dreams* movie, but it is a risky mantra for an organization to follow. In real organizational life, this target costing sequence makes more sense: first, find out what customers want, then what they are willing to pay, and then how much it will cost to provide those features, and then design the product/service according to those targets. Such a sequence is a much more tenable means for introducing new products/services that are most likely to have market acceptance and attractive financial outcomes. A target costing approach is one example of a process-oriented way to bridge the potential marketing and engineering gulf. The approach puts product/service designers, production/delivery systems, potential customers, and marketing decision-makers together at the start of a new product/service development initiative. In the end, cross-functional conversations are facilitated by this approach, leading to purposeful discussions pertaining to the cost efficacy of a product/service that is best checked before rolling out those products/services.

REFLECT: *Think of a person you have worked with (at your employer or in the community) whom you see as a bridge builder—one who connects people, processes, or strategies to enhance and further an endeavor. What did it feel like associating with them? How did they do what they did in building those bridges? Did those bridges provide a net benefit in your mind? Why and how?*

Recall some prior problematic issues/tensions related to one part of your organization not fully understanding, appreciating, or coordinating with another part. Recall the frustrations and the problems that resulted. Do you think they could have been mitigated or even avoided at an earlier juncture via a bridge builder? If so, how? If not, why not?

_____

_____

_____

_____

IDENTIFY: *Within your organization, think of a department or function that you are not a part of but that you rely on from time to time. Pick one where that periodic need for reliance, coordination, or integration could be improved. How might an ongoing bridge-building mindset be helpful in that regard? Could that bridge-building mindset be effective if it were simply an informal process of various parties periodically connecting, or would it be most helpful to develop a more formalized process (the target costing example was one good example of a specific process for a specific purpose)? Think carefully in this regard. Too many formalized processes can be counterproductive, but just the right ones for the right purposes can be very helpful. Identify one or two bridge-building opportunities that could be more formalized. Think of yourself as the designated bridge builder. Spec that role and the approach you would envision wanting to take in that regard.*

_____

_____

_____

_____

SHARE: *Connect with a managerial peer in the other organizational department or function that you believe would benefit from having a more reliable and robust bridge to your department or function. Without recrimination or blame, make the case for wanting a better bridge between the two. Garner their reaction and discuss. If there is agreement, share with them your thoughts about what you propose doing as someone interested in and volunteering to take the lead on such an initiative. Enlist their support and assistance. Be willing to shoulder the lead role, and be a partner in a purposeful, joint way.*

EVALUATE: *Generally, intraorganizational bridge building begins in informal ways. What did you do in that regard, and why? Was it effective, and why or why not? What would you do differently, and why? If you wanted to help other managers become effective bridge builders, how would you do that? Would you want to document some steps, to-dos, and processes? If so, strive to do so in conjunction with your colleague, aiming to codify a generalized and replicable approach. Was your bridge-building initiative a learning experience? If so, what did you learn, why is that important, and how has that made you a better manager?*

... ANOTHER CHAPTER 2 VIGNETTE ...

> **#7 *Hope and osmosis.***

Hope is not a strategy[24]

—Mark Greaney,
#1 *New York Times* Bestselling author of The Gray Man series

[... and yet ...]

[he] persisted in watering the fading flowers of hope.[25]

—Kevin Fedarko,
winner of National Outdoor Book Award

AFTER RIGOROUS AND robust planning, it is natural to then be hopeful that all goes well. Hopefulness is best thought of as an outcome of good planning, not an input to it. Hope should never be a substitute for analytics, sound thinking, broad perspectives, frank discussions, appropriately marshaled resources, and continuous monitoring of the planned and launched endeavor. Good planning also identifies prospective course correction indicators for prompting appropriate in-process corrective actions. And good planning involves brainstorming with colleagues about the nature of possible unwanted, unintended consequences and the mitigating steps to take.

I do not find many managers relying on hope as their primary organizational operating strategy, but I do see hope crop up in their thoughts regarding colleagues and direct reports. "I hope they will understand." "I hope they see the importance of that." "I hope they will be patient." "I hope they land that account." Well, there's an obvious question to ask yourself if you are thinking or hearing yourself say such things: "Have I done all I can do to help along those lines?" If the answer is no, it is time to address hope—be proactive and take action to increase the odds that those colleagues and direct reports will end up where you would like to see them end up. In our most objective moments, we know hope is not a valid strategy.

On a related front, have you heard of MBWA? Management by Walking Around, a.k.a. Management by Wandering Around. Many managers believe in it and see it as an important part of fulfilling their duty to be present. But is being physically present and being seen enough? Even a warm hello falls short of what's possible when you interact face-to-face with your direct reports. Believing that MBWA conveys and fosters caring, values, understanding, or connection is believing that osmosis is an effective interpersonal phenomenon, not just a biological or chemical one.[26] MBWA, without stopping, without knocking on someone's door to see if they have a moment to chat, is not connecting, caring, or conveying interest. In a virtual setting, lingering online after the meeting is over is usually time well spent for meaningfully connecting. In either setting, short, casual conversations with just a couple of simple questions—"What are you working on?" "How's it going?" "Do you have what you need?" "Do you have any questions that I might address?"—can supercharge the benefits of being out amongst one's direct reports and others. Offering encouragement, appreciation, and insights as to how they fit into the larger picture can be an important motivating exchange. And what did it take, a fifteen-minute exchange with two or three people during the day or the week? A small investment with potentially big returns. Don't rely on osmosis; it is not a valid managerial tool.

REFLECT: *In your job, have you ever found yourself using words like "hope," "wish," or "long for"? (Carefully think back over recent months.) If you have, and it was not in a frivolous, idiosyncratic way, in what specific context(s) did it surface in either your conversations or in your thinking? Was it more like wishing for something even without the necessary steps for the goal to come to fruition? Or closer to expecting something because you laid the groundwork for success?*

In your job, have you ever avoided or overlooked communicating to your direct reports the foundational norms, values, purpose, mission, or objectives you saw as important because you assumed they knew them, understood them, heard them from another source, and/or subscribed to them simply by having a certain amount of time in their current position? (Remember that osmosis is not a valid management tool!) In what arenas and for what issues can you see that additional clarity, specificity, and/or reinforcement might be beneficial to leave no doubt as to what you wanted them to know and do?

_____
_____
_____
_____
_____

IDENTIFY: *In the arena of "hope," what one or two hopes would benefit from additional planning so that appropriate steps could be delineated and taken, needed resources mustered, desired results stipulated, and progress monitored? Think about all the facets of your responsibilities that might include personnel, processes, systems, services, customers/clients, and other pertinent constituencies. Sketch out the details of how you best see converting* *any lingering hopes to specific plans and steps for a desired outcome.*

In the arena of "osmosis," what one or two norms, values, purposes, missions, or objectives have you been remiss in <u>explicitly</u> detailing and championing for your direct reports? Conceptualize an approach to making those more known and highlighted.

_____

_____

_____

_____

_____

SHARE: *Take a colleague to lunch. Share the inquiry you're engaging with through this book. Explain that hope generally fills/spans any gaps in planned tasks and that osmosis generally undergirds the avoidance of proactive discussions pertaining to the subtle but important aspects of priorities, values, and norms. With that introduction, do two things. First, share with them your own confessions in that regard and your ideas for replacing "hope" and "osmosis" with specific plans and proactive outreach. Then, invite them to be conscientious and honest in identifying the nature and extent of their reliance on hope and osmosis too. Ask your colleague what possibilities they see within their realm for setting aside hope and osmosis and stepping into concrete plans and outreach. Consider their reactions and feedback for modifying and improving your commitments for action on these two fronts.*

_____

_____

_____

_____

_____

EVALUATE: *Was it problematic to convert "hopes" into actionable plans and a targeted direction/outcome? If so, why? What might that suggest about your approach or your articulation of the object/subject of your previously identified hope? Have you been intentional in becoming less reliant on osmosis as a conscious or subconscious management tool? Are you engaged in MBWA but with a willingness to stop and engage with personnel authentically and substantively along the way? If not, why not? Have you availed yourself of other organizational opportunities and channels for making various things explicit—for example, using such things as previously scheduled meetings, newsletters, and/or frequent "Top of the Mind" or "Reminders for All of Us" email missives? If not, why not?*

_____
_____
_____
_____

... A FINAL CHAPTER 2 VIGNETTE ...

> **#8 *Have a freedom fund.***

[His] moral compass was trying to steer his body to get involved, but his brain was fighting back.[27]

—MARK GREANEY,
#1 *New York Times* Bestselling author of The Gray Man series

A SENIOR EXECUTIVE responsible for his firm's international operations told me the advice he had regularly shared with the rising managers and executives he mentored. Amongst his other more administratively and technically oriented pieces of advice was this: "You need to have a 'go to h**l fund.'" The message was not a subtle one. He was saying that there might be a time when others ask or expect them to do something—or not do something—that they felt violated their personal values. Clearly, organizations have protocols and chains of command and perhaps even an ombudsperson, all intended to help in such troublesome situations. And yet, there may come a moment when the best course of action is for a person to simply leave—walk away.

There are too many known accounts of managers misbehaving to believe that it cannot happen in your own organization. It can. I'm sure the managers at MiniScribe Corporation did not map out a career strategy of shipping bricks in hard-drive packaging to boost sales and conceal inventory shortfalls from senior management.[28] I'm sure the engineers at Ford Motor Company did not intend to react to a cost-benefit analysis by compromising the safety measures that would have mitigated the possibility of an exploding Pinto gas tank if hit in a crash in just the wrong way.[29] There must have been someone at Theranos, Inc., who knew the company's revolutionary blood testing devices did not perform as promised, if at all, in contradiction to the story being repeatedly told by its fundraising CEO at the time.[30] Yet, in any of these cases, did employees raise their voices? If not, what prevented them? If they did, were they heard?

It is naïve to think that managers might never find themselves under pressure from an ethical dilemma or unreasonable boss. Such pressures can stem from ordinary factors like mortgage payments or rent, childcare or college tuition, saving for retirement, or caregiving for an ailing parent. Financial pressures are real and can prompt behaviors that are rationalized, justified, and ultimately internalized and acted upon. And in the light of day, with no attendant pressures, it might have been clearer and easier to say no.

So what is a "go to h**l" fund? It is a freedom fund. It is a bank account of don't-stay dollars. It is move-on money set aside equal to four to six months of living expenses. It is money intended to alleviate the immediate financial pressures that might prompt, or even necessitate, you to stay and go along with something that you seriously are not comfortable with. The fund is a simple means for not feeling trapped—for giving yourself some degree of freedom.

A bit of digression is useful. My historical noninterest in horses has recently turned to curiosity and a desire to learn more about them because I now have two granddaughters who love them and a close friend who is a horse vet. One tidbit of horse training information that I have learned is pertinent here. Well-respected horse trainers who opt for training and taming horses by means other than the bronco-busting, show-them-who-is-boss techniques of the Wild West typically work with a wild or unruly horse in a round pen. As one nationally known trainer states, "The round pen has no corners where a horse can get trapped, so despite the fact that it's a small space, it allows them to keep moving. They always have an escape route."[31] A freedom fund provides the symbolic round corners of your work context that enable you to not feel trapped when your situation becomes untenable due to ethical conflicts or boredom, stagnation, or unappreciation.

REFLECT: *Scenario #1: It is easy to think of encountering ethical dilemmas as something that happens elsewhere—i.e., "not at my organization." But there are too many stories where it has happened in contexts that people thought unlikely. Not all dilemmas make the cover of national papers or trail across CNN's ticker. Ethical dilemmas come in all sizes. How prepared are you for that possibility? Are there espoused norms and values in your organization that do not quite seem to matter as much when financial results are lagging projections, pending deadlines are looming, or critical customer/client/donor accounts are in danger of leaving? Have you been asked to do something, even something small, that carried a rationalization that just did not feel right? In hindsight, are you aware of conversations that caused you unease? If so, how did you react? Did you provide pushback? Ignore it? Bring it to someone else's attention? Think about quitting? If the latter, did you feel that was too big a step to take? Was it financially daunting to think about such a move? If you'd had a freedom fund, might you have left? Why or why not?*

Scenario #2: Have you ever been frequently bored by your work, consistently unappreciated, or disappointed by a boss that you did not respect? Such situations might also benefit from having a freedom fund. With such a fund, you might not feel chained/trapped to an organization, role, or boss who was energy-draining and not life-giving—you could make a move. Take note of what your heart and conscience are whispering (or shouting) regarding either scenario.

IDENTIFY: *Carefully assess the likelihood of scenario #1 or #2 occurring. What would it take to lessen the accompanying dependence, discomfort, victimhood, or never-resolved disagreement? Might a freedom fund be part of the answer? If so, think about how much money you would need to put aside and what sort of situational tripwire(s) would cause you to need it.*

SHARE: *Confide in a friend your interest in establishing a freedom fund. Share with that person the actual and envisioned freedom it would give you. Listen to their reaction to make sure you are not moving into the realm of operating with unhealthy stress, anxiety, worry, or even fear. Your friend is probably not a counselor, but they can provide a reality/reasonableness check for you. Do they see the merits of such an approach? Why or why not?*

EVALUATE: *A financial safety net is a good idea. Mergers, downsizing, and restructuring can happen in any organization. A financial cushion is wise to have for these common organizational possibilities. Importantly and in addition, the two scenarios noted earlier can also trigger the need for funds. Did you establish a freedom fund for those possibilities—with enough savings or a plan for contributing to it regularly? If not, why not? (Don't be guilty of the ostrich syndrome—i.e., I won't be put in a compromising situation, or I'll always have enough money for unforeseen circumstances.) If you did establish such a fund, has it provided independence? (Not detachment but less dependency.) If it has, good. If it hasn't, why not? Is it not enough? Are you fearful you couldn't make such a move?*

_____
_____
_____
_____
_____

CHAPTER 3

Ideas for Action: Diagnostic-Focused
[vignettes #9–#17]

> **#9 *Focus on focus.***

Our focus continually fights distractions, both inner and outer.[32]

—DANIEL GOLEMAN,
author of the number one international
bestseller *Emotional Intelligence*

IN *THE MYTH* *of Excellence*, the authors emphasize focus: "The best companies have a strategy for dominating (i.e., being world-class) on one of five attributes of product, price, access, experience, and service . . ." Striving for all five will not lead to excellence. Instead, they argue, companies should not attempt to be world-class on more than one attribute, striving to be ". . . differentiating on a second and being at industry par on the remaining three."[33]

My experience with all types of organizations and individual managers points to a similar conclusion: the importance of a focus on focus. You and your organization cannot be world-class in everything you do. And that is not a judgment, an excuse, or a rationalization for being derelict or shoddy on anything.

Companies have increasingly outsourced aspects of their enterprise. The economy's digital transformation easily illustrates how focus gives rise to doing what you do well (as an organization) and outsourcing what you do not. For example, software as a service (SaaS) integrates functions such as payroll (which might be assigned to Paycom Software, Inc.), customer/client interfacing (which can be managed through Salesforce, Inc.), and the integration of an organization's overall information systems to SAP SE. Some retailers and mail-order companies find it advantageous to outsource warehousing and delivery to FedEx Corporation. On-site, ServiceMaster Company provides facilities cleaning for many organizations, and Securitas AB is often an organization's security provider of choice. Such focused companies do what they do—and do it well—so other organizations do not have to, providing them with the opportunity to focus on what they were created to do.

In general, a focus on focus at the organizational level often involves outsourcing noncore tasks to other companies for whom those tasks are core. For many managers, noncore tasks divert time, money, attention, and personnel that could be more productively used elsewhere. As an example, consider Rolls Royce NA, a manufacturer of jet engines and provider of services related to those engines. To facilitate their managers' identification of outsourcing opportunities, the company asks their managers to view what they do along two dimensions:

- the criticality of the task performed (or the component part produced) to the unique nature of the product/service they provide, and
- the competitiveness with which the task (or component part produced) is provided.

For Rolls Royce NA, the "criticality" dimension pertains to the role played by an engine's component parts or a particular internal operating process in creating a valued differential advantage for the company in the marketplace. The "competitiveness" dimension highlights the construct of cost leadership pertaining to a process or component part. (It is my belief that this dimension also applies to quality leadership [or the lack thereof].) The internal activities that have a small effect on competitiveness and are also low in criticality are outsourced. Those that are highly critical but that the organization is not able to do competitively are outsourced too, but with stringent contractual arrangements or via joint ventures, strategic alliances, or formal partnerships to protect the criticality (i.e., proprietary) aspect. Those processes or component parts that are low on the criticality dimension but contribute greatly to the firm's competitive position remain in-house but could be outsourced at any moment if an attractive supplier or partner becomes known that provides the process or component part for less cost and/or higher quality.

Only those in-house activities/processes and component-parts production that the organization does exceedingly well on the competitiveness dimension of cost and quality leadership and are highly critical to the firm's distinctiveness are not outsourced. Specifically, it is this latter combination where the company achieves a highly competitive capability to do something that is highly critical to the company's distinctive services and/or products that becomes the core focus of the company.

A focus on focus at the individual manager level, in my opinion, dictates that individuals think in terms of developing a portfolio of T-shaped skills[34] over time. The top of the T represents a person's breadth of knowledge and collaborative capabilities, while the trunk of the T signifies a person's depth of expertise in their chosen field. "Breadth *and* depth are key."[35]

Initially, aspiring managers have a natural focus on developing depth—an expertise for which they become known and in which they excel. As a young manager is tapped with increasing and varied managerial opportunities, that initial expertise is retained, but it is no longer the focus. The breadth of exposure to other facets of the organization now takes center stage. Financial experts have risen to become corporate CEOs as have marketing gurus and IT specialists. Artillery officers, as well as infantry officers, have risen to become US Army generals. Economists and accountants have risen to become deans at prestigious business schools. Historians and literary scholars have become university presidents. The best of those gravitating to such elevated managerial positions knew, to some extent, what they didn't know and focused on learning what they needed to know, complementing that knowledge with a reliable team of experts. Successful managers develop T-shaped capabilities that enable them to lead, coordinate, inspire, and focus their collective efforts toward the mission of the organization or unit they head.

REFLECT: *What handful of things at work would you most personally want to focus on, and why? Do those desired foci align with what your organization needs or asks of you? If not, why not? In what way(s) are you distracted from them? What are the root causes of those distractions? What one task that you or your department are responsible for do you believe could be done better (or more appropriately) by another? What harms and benefits would accrue to you and/or your organization if that possibility was given to another?*

_____

_____

_____

_____

IDENTIFY: *Formulate an approach to eliminating or minimizing the major distractions you personally encounter at work. Also, what due diligence steps make sense for exploring the possible outsourcing (internally or externally) of that one task you believe could be done better (or more appropriately) by another? In both instances, make sure the approaches are actionable and that you have considered some of the possible unintended consequences that might result and that may warrant proactive mitigating actions. Do the approaches you have crafted foster a potentially significant beneficial outcome in your mind? If not, perhaps it is not a bold enough approach with substantial and sustainable value-added potential. Remember, doing less of something creates the potential for doing more of something and/or doing something better.*

_____
_____
_____
_____

SHARE: *Look for an opportunity to explain to a colleague the nature of the distractions you face, the approach you want to take to eradicate (or minimize) them, and the possible ripple effects that might result. What is their reaction? Are distractions an issue for that colleague too? Why or why not? Do you both share some of the same thoughts pertaining to the root cause(s) of distractions? If so, might that point to a systemic organizational factor needing to be surfaced and addressed at the organizational level? If distractions were to be reduced or eliminated, what would be the specific beneficial results that would accrue to you and to the organization?*

Share with that colleague your idea for a value-added task to outsource (either internally or externally). Be prepared to identify carefully and comprehensively the specific value that would accrue to the organization from such a move. Did your colleague see the merits? Why or why not? Was your idea too threatening or seen as fraught with negative implications? If so, perhaps that is a confidential conversation worth having.

_____
_____
_____
_____
_____

EVALUATE: *If you acted on striving to eliminate personal distractions from your desired foci, were you able to reduce (or eliminate) some of the more frequent and significant distractions? If not, why not? Can and should you try again? Were you more productive or effective at your job with those distractions gone? If not, why not? Were they not the true root cause of your time, energy, or attention being siphoned away from your core responsibilities and/or your core work-related passion? Were there any negative ripple effects from you having eliminated/ avoided those distractions? If so, what, and is that okay or in need of remedying? Do you have a case that can be made at the organizational level for some systemic root causes of recurring distractions being addressed? If so, consider how best to do that because of the potential value to be gained.*

Did you find the topic of potential outsourcing (either internally or externally) too toxic to meaningfully surface and discuss? Why or why not? If it was too toxic, do the underlying reasons warrant discussion and addressing? Were they fear-based? Turf-protection-based? Prone to precedent-setting? If it was not too toxic, did the perceived upside outweigh the perceived downside, and is it more likely than not that your proposal will be accepted and beneficial?

... ANOTHER CHAPTER 3 VIGNETTE ...

> **#10 *Paint the picture.***

If you want him to do it, you've got to change the picture of the world inside his head.[36]

—Robert Penn Warren,
first poet laureate of the United States

WIDE EYES, EXCITED smiles, and stunned silence told him he had captivated the employees in his audience. In his hands, he held a magazine cover with a bold headline that celebrated his company's success. Dated five years into the future, the cover mimicked that of a news magazine like *TIME*. It was only a mockup, but it painted a powerful image of the company's future as he envisioned it. As the new CEO of a large organization, he had found a way to enroll his colleagues in his own vision of the company's future. He did not stop there. He went on to detail the content he envisioned in the article, chronicling the important aspects of the organization that had propelled it to such acclaim.

It was unlikely that a general news magazine such as *TIME* would ever run such a feature on any organization. But he had made his point. By the end of this organization's retreat, he had presented coworkers with a memorable image, a concrete picture, and illuminating details. He had effectively communicated all that, enabling others to see, relate to, comprehend, and embrace where the organization was headed and how it was to get there.

I heard this story from a colleague down the hall who was researching effective means for leading strategic organizational change. She interviewed this CEO about how he communicated his vision for the organization to the hundreds of people in its different divisions. His response was that story.

Many of my colleagues and I were so inspired by this means for communicating a corporate vision that we have used it as an assignment in some of our management development seminars. It is fascinating to see managers from a single organization craft magazine cover mockups touting their organization for one or more accomplishments or characteristics. The task of fashioning a visual image and related story content is an effective and provocative means for conveying a clear message that might otherwise be limited to glittering generalities, amorphous impressions, or clichéd slogans.

Put simply, a vision should paint a vivid picture. A clearly communicated organizational vision accomplishes so much. It points to a desired future, sharpens focus, denotes direction, helps arbitrate debates, rallies resources, motivates movement along high-priority pathways, and defines success. Perhaps most importantly, painting a picture provides a touchstone for assessing when an organization is on track and when it is in danger of losing one or more of the important components of progress toward its envisioned future.

REFLECT: *What do you see when you envision the future of your organizational unit, department, or work team? Take a wide view. Avoid a narrow "soda-straw view" of the who, what, when, where, and how aspects of direction and destination. Envision where you want your organizational unit, department, or work team to be in three to five years. What characteristics must it possess to get there? What are some key hallmarks of that envisioned, successful future (list four to six adjectives that best apply)? What publication cover, website homepage, or video news* segment could be powerfully used to capture the essence of what you envision? Can you picture it? Could you paint it? Are you willing to present it?

_____
_____
_____
_____

IDENTIFY: *Who at work, at home, or among your friends could help with the needed artwork, design, graphics, editing, or writing to put together the magazine cover (or web page proclamation) you envision? If you prefer, produce a short video, perhaps even a mock news segment touting that future. What upcoming work venue provides an appropriate opportunity for unveiling and using your cover or video? What follow-on activities would be needed to push the idea(s) embedded in the cover or the video toward fruition?*

_____
_____
_____
_____

SHARE: *Craft a mockup cover, related story, short video news segment, or web post and share it with a coworker. Be prepared to answer their questions related to why you are doing this, what you hope to achieve, when you want it completed, and how you plan to use it. Was your coworker excited or intrigued by your idea? Why or why not? Garner and consider their suggestions. Plan your implementation and execute it, sharing it with your targeted* *audience in the most powerful way you can envision.*

___

___

___

___

EVALUATE: *How did it go? Did your audience get it? Like it? Were people ho-hum or energized? What resonated with them? Why? In retrospect, could you have done it better? If so, how? Does it make sense to repeat the exercise as a downstream galvanizing reminder? Should you follow up with version 2.0 in six or twelve months to powerfully chronicle progress and continue to point to the desired future? If not, why not, and are there aspects of the vision or organization that should be addressed to make it more conducive to moving toward an exciting, envisioned future? To what extent did the production of the cover or video require you to think concretely and specifically about what, when, why, where, and how pertaining to that envisioned future? If not, perhaps the visuals and story were not as inspiring or as concrete as they could have been. If so, consider a later, second try.*

___

___

___

___

...ANOTHER CHAPTER 3 VIGNETTE...

> **#11 Learn from "stay interviews."**

... if people can figure out who they are, they will no longer wonder what they should do.[37]

—TODD PIERCE,
former champion bareback bronco rodeo rider
and current CEO and founder of Riding High Ministries

ONE OF THE frequent, final encounters managers have with a departing employee is an exit interview. All too often, however, those interviews are mostly perfunctory, lacking depth on the part of both parties and generally inconsequential as viable inputs for a subsequent organizational or managerial change. If an employee is leaving with positive feelings, an exit interview is mostly a fond farewell, with best wishes and a few words of thanks and appreciation. If the employee is leaving with not-so-positive sentiments, at worst, the exchange is a bitter and final lodging-of-complaints gripe session, and at best, a civil recounting of shortcomings that might ultimately warrant follow-up by the interviewer.

In a recent conversation with a senior executive, she described her practice of holding periodic "stay interviews" with key direct reports who were not leaving. What a great idea! I believe such meetings are best decoupled from annual performance review meetings. They provide a rich opportunity to ask, in a non-assessment context, questions such as "What keeps you here?" "What's the best part of your job, and why do you enjoy that?" "What could be improved or clarified about the processes and responsibilities associated with your job?" "How can I help you grow professionally?" "What do you aspire to be doing personally and professionally in five years, and why?"[38] Such questions are (1) best given in advance to the interviewee to prompt their thoughtful preparation and (2) aimed at ascertaining what aspects of work most resonate with the employee and what currently tapped and untapped aspects of that employee's truest aspirations are important for the organization to align with and access. "Stay interviews" surface meaningful opportunities for managers to connect with direct reports more powerfully—not just with their heads (knowledge) and hands (capabilities) but also with their hearts (aspirations and passions). Knowing and then finding ways to tap an employee's aspirations can provide an organization with a richer, more sustainable springboard for fueling an employee's pursuit of excellence, growth, and commitment.

For young managers who do not have direct reports, it can be valuable to ask such stay-type questions of themselves and/or their peers. When asked of yourself, the answers to such questions serve to crystallize goals, highlight the merits of redirected focus and efforts, and help in prioritizing opportunities to seize and distractions to avoid. When asked of peers, the answers contribute to deepened familiarities and friendships and strengthened collaborations, and they provide a foundation for establishing a shared organizational culture.

REFLECT: *Why did you come to work for your current employer? Why are you still there? What do you like best about your work and employer? What do you like least about your work and employer? In this latter regard, have you or your job and/or your employer changed? Were you unable or unwilling to change in concert with any job or employer changes, and if so, why? If you have changed, what is it that you now most want in your job and from your employer? Is that possible where you are, and if* not, why not? If it is possible, what happens next? (Is your freedom fund in place [recall vignette #8]? If not, would now be a good time to start building it?)

IDENTIFY: *Over time, how will you need to change, if at all, to continue to find your work and employer appealing? In the same spirit, what will become important for you to have in your work responsibilities and from your employer so that you can become the best employee and best manager you can be? What do you need to do in the next several months to be prepared for where you want to be? How might your boss be helpful to you in that regard? Be prepared to describe the value you want to provide your employer as a result of becoming the manager you want to become.*

SHARE: *Perhaps it is best to share your thoughts on the above questions you asked yourself with a nonwork friend. Ask them to be honest when you ask them: Are my expectations realistic? Am I too self-centric in my expectations and potential requests? Will I be offering something of value to my employer? Would you want me to work for you? Why or why not?*

EVALUATE: *Based upon your refined thinking from the vetting above, schedule a stay interview with your boss. Similarly, hold stay interviews with your direct reports. After completing both types, analyze how they went. After speaking with your boss, are you more or less inclined to stay? Why? Based on your stay interviews with your direct reports, are there some new and actionable ideas that you can now pursue to keep your best employees? If so, seize the moment. If not, are there other questions you should have asked them? If so, note those for next time.*

. . . ANOTHER CHAPTER 3 VIGNETTE . . .

> **#12** *One bad constituent-facing employee encounter can ruin a relationship.*

. . . the things you put in your head are there forever.[39]

—CORMAC MCCARTHY,
winner of the Pulitzer Prize for Fiction

IT WAS A big deal. It was a significant birthday event, and the honoree had specifically requested the celebratory family meal to be Sunday brunch at a fancy downtown hotel. We anticipated the event for days. Finally, the date arrived. The lobby of the hotel was magnificently decorated for its upscale clientele. Four different lavish food lines were garlanded with fresh flowers and offered multiple options. A tuxedoed string quartet was playing softly in the background, and a tall-hatted trio of chefs were standing by, ready to serve and explain.

As we approached the welcome station for seating, we noticed the semi-disheveled, frown-faced, obviously not-happy-to-be-working hostess at that post. She was our first official point of contact for the entire occasion. We were fourth in line. The hostess was answering the ringing phone and had two waitstaff standing nearby to seat customers. The hostess was brusque to people on the phone. She curtly asked (it was more of an order) those of us in line to be patient and ignored the two waitstaff members. This lasted for what seemed like a long and uncomfortable ten minutes. We never once saw her smile, offer an apology, or utter a kind word to anyone. She was the *hostess from hell*.

In a matter of minutes, she had managed to deflate our buoyant mood, burst our hopeful image of the brunch experience, alter the pleasant ambiance of the place, and become the focal point of our far-less-than-positive observations. The hotel had gone to great lengths to provide a wonderful brunch in a wonderful setting but had failed miserably to pick the right person as hostess and to separate the hostess tasks from the reservation-taking phone tasks. A handsomely attired host or elegantly dressed hostess, either one ready with a welcoming word and an engaging smile, could have so effortlessly and positively reinforced all the hotel had tried to create for its customers. As it was, we ended up noting that she may have missed her calling: a grumpy reform school headmistress. In the end, we had a great birthday celebration, but with no contribution from the *hostess from hell.*

We probably all have stories of less-than-pleasant encounters with a disengaged DMV administrator, an unhelpful customer service representative, or a curt store clerk. Just in the past six months, I have encountered a rude and unhelpful propane gas company helpline person, a smug and condescending salesperson for a home improvements contractor, and a bank back-office person who even after an hour on the phone could not tell me why one of my deposits had not been accepted. I haven't forgotten them, just as you no doubt remember similar experiences. When we remember them, we remember their employer as much as the individual. And that's important.

Interactions between employees and various constituents are of enormous importance, with each interaction potentially benefitting or poisoning the relationship. Clearly, the key for employers is picking and equipping the right people for those constituent-facing positions and sparing no effort to prepare them for the countless opportunities per day to make a good first impression (and additional impressions!) on behalf of their employer.

REFLECT: *As a customer/client/donor, recall a time when you were either disappointed or upset by an interaction with an organization's designated point-of-contact person. What could (should) that person have done to interact with you better? Even if you lost your temper or conveyed your anger, what could (should) they have done to diffuse the emotion and adequately address your issue?*

As a manager, have you experienced an encounter with a disgruntled constituent? If so, recall the details of that situation. What could (should) you have done differently or better in response to that customer/client/donor? Did your organization proactively and adequately prepare you for customer/client/donor encounters? If so, what did they do well in that regard? If not, why not? What was missing?

_____
_____
_____
_____

IDENTIFY: *What one improvement could be made in how your organizational unit conducts its first interaction with an internal or external constituent (e.g., another organizational department, a customer, client, donor, supplier, community member, regulator, contractor, etc.)? In that vein, what guidance can you provide for that improvement to be successfully and wholeheartedly embraced? What monitoring means might you need to operationalize to provide assurance that that guidance is embraced, followed, and effective?*

_____
_____

SHARE: *In the spirit of seeking insight, consider going undercover (or enlisting the aid of a colleague from another department). Call or email several of the most likely constituent-facing personnel in your unit. Ask them some realistic, pertinent questions. Ask them for frequently requested assistance. Ask them for information. Ask them for instruction or explanation. How did they do? What needs to be done better? How might you refine the guidance and monitoring you first proposed? Is there an organizational benefit to be garnered from a wider approach to constituent-facing guidance and monitoring? If so, collaborate with a small group of colleagues on how best to propose it to your bosses.*

EVALUATE: *On an ongoing basis, stay vigilant regarding your organizational unit's constituent-facing encounters. Are there instances for celebrating outstanding examples of what you are seeking? If so, make it happen. Stay abreast of what your constituent-facing personnel are encountering in that role. Be responsive to the evolving nature of those encounters. Partner with the best of your people for ideas regarding the orientation for new hires, the ongoing incentives for maintaining excellence, and how your unit can become known internally and even externally as a best-practices unit in this arena. And don't forget to celebrate* *and thank those who do it well.*

... ANOTHER CHAPTER 3 VIGNETTE ...

> **#13 *20/80 or 80/20?***

It's what we call . . . a weapon of mass disruption.[40]

—DAVID BALDACCI,
novelist whose sales are in the millions

RULES OF THUMB are not perfect. They can, however, be helpful as general guidelines or norms. For example, it is often stated that if you drive no more than five miles per hour over the speed limit, you'll not be stopped. Or that it is best to arrive at the airport two hours before your flight in case of long security lines. Or that it's best to "let sleeping dogs lie."

Consider the fact that 20 percent of a workweek is the equivalent of one day, and 80 percent of the workweek is four days. As a rule of thumb, if the equivalent of one day a week (i.e., 20 percent) is spent on customers/clients/donors who generate 80 percent of your revenues, and they are truly happy, chances are you are doing something right. In essence, you are receiving a large benefit from a comparatively lower level of time and effort. Moreover, if four days of your workweek (i.e., 80 percent) are spent on customers/clients/donors who generate only 20 percent of your revenues, happy or unhappy, chances are you are doing something they do not value, or something is wrong.[41] In this instance, your time and effort are disproportionately higher than the benefits received.

Similarly, and internally, if one day of your workweek (i.e., 20 percent) is spent dealing with 80 percent of your direct reports, and they are truly happy, chances are you are doing something right. If the equivalent of four days of your workweek (i.e., 80 percent) are spent dealing with 20 percent of your direct reports, happy or unhappy, chances are you are doing something they do not value, or something wrong.

For the internal or external constituency, the "something" that is *happening right* is most likely when systems are working and aligned, expectations are mutual, and positive outcomes have been achieved from the time and attention you are investing. In contrast, the "something" that is *happening wrong* or that is not valued is when systems are not working or aligned, expectations are disparate, and positive outcomes have not been delivered.

For the external customer/client/donor constituency, it is likely that the systems to focus on to address the "something" that is wrong pertain to service, distribution, pricing, reliability, communications, quality, partnering, or some combination of these. Regarding expectations, it is best for them to be explicit and mutually understood—for example, making revenue terms, schedules, special considerations, and respective responsibilities explicit, clear, and acknowledged. If outcomes and deliverables are not what they should or could be, it is important to revisit how things get done and your delegation choices, the flow of information, time management priorities, pricing, and the process for addressing problems. There may be a customer/client/donor who will never be totally satisfied no matter how you try to address their complaint(s). You or your organization may need to decide to walk away from them, choosing not to serve them, or they may opt out if you made it clear as to what you can and can't provide.

In the personnel arena, the systems to focus on for improvement are likely those that pertain to compensation, performance reviews, communications, advancement, hiring, training, and/or recognition. Regarding expectations, it is again best to make them explicit and check everyone's understanding of job responsibilities, job opportunities, incentives, and their line of sight to see how their work helps the organization. If outcomes and deliverables are not what they should or could be, it is important to revisit the systems aspects noted above as well as your delegation-of-tasks choices, time-management priorities, and the nature of the personnel problems you most frequently encounter. There is frequently some point at which a problematic employee becomes toxic to others and to an organization's mission. With proper adherence to all regulations and after good-faith efforts to rectify the personnel problem situation, it may be mutually beneficial for both parties to part ways.

REFLECT: *In general, what minority of internal or external constituent-related issues (e.g., 20 percent) occupy most of your workweek time (e.g., 80 percent)? Is there a commensurate level of benefit that comes from that level of attention? If not, why not? Need it to be out of balance? If so, why? Is there something about the nature of the issue that demands most of your time, or is there something about you (e.g., skills, interest, proximity, etc.) that leads to most of your time being spent in that direction? Be honest. Conversely, what is it about those internal or external constituents from whom the organization garners substantial benefits (e.g., 80 percent) but who only require a minimum amount of your time, effort, and attention (e.g., 20 percent)? Is there something in those relationships that is replicable? If so, what? Is there something in how you interact with them that is key? If so, what?*

_____

_____

_____

_____

IDENTIFY: *Pick one of the issues or constituents that you identified as frequently occupying a disproportionate amount of your attention. What are the specifics of that issue or constituent that are most demanding? What ideas can you generate for how to address those demands better? Is it a delegation approach? A need to be better informed? An education need? As best as you can preliminarily do, flesh out the details of an approach or the contents of a conversation that seeks to remedy the disproportionately demanding nature of the issue or constituent.*

_____

_____

_____

_____

SHARE: *Share with a trusted colleague the disproportionate scenario you have identified and the ideas you have for remedying it. Do they also regularly encounter a similarly imbalanced situation? If so, what have they done to try to remedy it? Did it work? Why or why not? What do they think of your idea(s)? Might they be able to support you as you fine-tune and pursue your idea(s)? Enumerate the benefits you believe will come from rectifying the unfavorable imbalance you have identified between time/attention versus benefits received.*

_____

_____

_____

_____

EVALUATE: *After several weeks, have your efforts been successful to some extent? If so, to what extent? What more needs to be done? If your efforts have been unsuccessful, why? Here, it might be helpful to share the disappointing outcome with a trusted colleague for insights and suggestions. "Business as usual" is not an empowering mantra, nor often merited. Think of all you could be doing more positively, more purposefully, and more expansively if you were to be able to shift a significant amount of time and attention each workweek from problematic issues/constituents to more enjoyable, value-added endeavors. Many, if not most, recurring problems are rectifiable and need not continue.*

_____
_____
_____
_____

. . . ANOTHER CHAPTER 3 VIGNETTE . . .

> **#14 *Regularly perform an assumptions audit.***

*You have to do some deconstruction
to do some reconstruction.*[42]

—PETE NELSON,
host of the television show *Treehouse Masters*

IN OUR AGE of high-velocity change, managers prepare themselves as best they can for the changing environment they are likely to encounter. Diligent managers read, learn, explore, extrapolate, and consider possibilities with an open mind. There are some, however, who take the ostrich approach—figuratively sticking their head in the sand and hoping they will not have to deal with significant change. For some of those managers, a "run-the-clock-out" strategy might work. It won't work, though, for any manager seeking to make a lasting contribution and maintain a significant career. The need for change will always arise regarding one or more of the following: customer/client/donor needs and preferences, technology to assist, employee talent to tap, competitors to monitor, opportunities to seize, reliable suppliers/affiliates to cultivate, and pitfalls to guard against.

It seems likely that Eastman Kodak Company and Polaroid Corporation assumed they had the camera market captured—who would have thought phones would become the new cameras? It seems likely that Yellow Cab companies throughout the United States assumed their competition would come from start-up cab companies, not citizens with a few spare hours to drive around town in their own cars for a company called Uber Technologies, Inc., or Lyft, Inc. I wonder if the PGA Tour (Professional Golf Association) ever anticipated the birth of the competitor LIV Golf group.[43] There are countless other examples of a shifting organizational landscape that, at least for many, was assumed to be not possible or at least not likely. Did traditional car dealers see vending-machine-like car purchases (Carvana Co.) coming? Did large department stores see personalized online clothes shoppers (Stitch Fix or MTailor) coming? Did traditional optometrist offices see economical at-home virtual eye exams and glasses to try at home (Warby Parker, Inc.) coming?

While managers must anticipate and face a steady wind of organizational change, people in general also want something that is immutable, less likely to change, dependable, and foundational that can be counted on as steadfast. Thus, the paradox—expecting change and desiring more certainty, not less. Perhaps both can comfortably coexist. Perhaps different managers have different foci for what and where they can embrace change versus what and where they would like to have things stay steady and constant.

One effective means for surfacing, evaluating, and consensually moving forward as a management team in the face of change is to periodically engage in an assumptions audit.[44] Such an undertaking simply begins with two or three organizational managers brainstorming as to the assumptions they see embedded in the values, beliefs, norms, protocols, and exogenous forces they each can identify as part of their own thinking. A robust array of assumptions can come to light as they challenge one another in a constructive and pointed manner. That subset of managers can also constructively work with another subset to clarify and codify a final inventory of managerial or organizational assumptions. Next, the final array of assumptions can be presented in a survey-type format to a larger group of pertinent managers. That instrument would simply ask each manager to denote, for each assumption, if it should be (1) kept, (2) dropped, or (3) modified for their collective going-forward planning purposes. And then, those results are aggregated. The aggregated views establish a basis for more effective ensuing planning discussions. Such discussions will be more effective because the aggregated results will:

- provide a nonthreatening, objectified means and basis for surfacing, questioning, and discussing long-held views,
- facilitate action-oriented discussions based on the three possible assumptions response categories,
- help build commitment to proposed organizational changes springing from any emergent consensus regarding assumptions to "drop" and "modify,"
- help in socializing new managers as to some of the organization's key planning foundations,
- help planning discussions to stay on track, not derailed by a vocal minority,
- establish degrees of freedom for the planning process by identifying those historical assumptions that can be set aside or modified,
- point to parts of the planning process and outcomes that warrant strengthening because of a consensus to "keep" certain assumptions,
- increase the odds of being able to implement significant change as opposed to only modest, incremental change intended to be acceptable to many parties without knowing what one another's key assumptions were,
- clarify and affirm an organization's shared values and beliefs, and
- shorten the overall planning process due to the substantial elimination of ongoing debates and compromises springing from differences of opinion that have already largely surfaced and been evaluated.

We all harbor managerial and organizational assumptions. It may have been a while since you concretely considered yours, or you may not know what your colleagues' assumptions are. A periodic assumptions audit can bring those to light, facilitating a positive and proactive shared understanding of one another.

REFLECT: *For a specific aspect of your organizational involvement, what "certainties" in your mind are tantamount to unchallenged assumptions? Which of those unchallenged assumptions are possibly unwarranted? For example, is bigger assumed to be better? Is more investment the assumed basis for solving a problem? Is the best talent assumed to be available only from the outside? These are but a few examples of issues that might now be undergirded by unchallenged assumptions that, once established, have been perpetuated. What avowed assumptions have you heard others express that seem to have fueled their preferences and decision-making? Also, what assumptions do you have that warrant highlighting? Be as complete as you can be. Are you a bit surprised by the nature and extensiveness of some of the assumptions you have been able to inventory? If so, that is testimony to how they take hold and can, over time, play an unexamined role in decision-making.*

_____
_____
_____
_____

IDENTIFY: *Using the list of assumptions you have identified on your own, craft a questionnaire that simply asks respondents whether they believe it is important to continue to hold onto that* *planning/operating assumption, modify it, or eliminate it. Allow space for respondents to add any other pertinent assumptions that occur to them.*

SHARE: *With a proper introduction to what you are attempting to do, ask an appropriate colleague or two to complete your questionnaire and add any additional assumptions they believe are embedded in the organization and in their own managerial thinking. Review their additions. Compare their questionnaire responses to yours. Ask for their reactions to the case you made for an assumptions audit and the process by which you propose doing it for the organization.*

EVALUATE: *How are the questionnaire results of your colleagues similar and dissimilar to yours and to each other? Do the dissimilarities point to the need for an important organizational conversation, and why or why not? If your organization has had an influx of new personnel, chances are that the set of shared organizational assumptions has become less shared. That is not necessarily a bad thing. It simply means that decision-makers are not operating from a shared institutional basis. Evaluate whether* *it is time for your organization to revisit those bases and, if so, the potential benefits from doing an assumptions audit as part of that endeavor.*

_____
_____
_____
_____
_____

... ANOTHER CHAPTER 3 VIGNETTE ...

> **#15 *Subject your KPIs to a behavioral audit.***

Not everything that can be counted counts, and not everything that counts can be counted.[45]

—William Bruce Cameron,
professor of sociology

"HOW ARE WE doing?" is perhaps the most asked question, whether implicitly or explicitly, by those responsible for the performance of an organizational unit, product line, regional territory, or service line. Strategies, goals, plans, and tactics occupy much of the time, talents, and energies of managers. Such foci must be translatable and assessable by the results achieved. Thus, part of what management must do is operationalize the concept of desired results into measurable constructs. This is done in the context of an embraced strategy, articulated goal, preliminary plan, and a portfolio of anticipated operating tactics. Because results are seldom instantaneous or totally observable, it is imperative that managers also develop intermediate monitoring means and indicators for assessing progress toward desired results.

I once asked a top executive of a major automotive parts company how he keeps his finger on the pulse of his North American operations, which consisted of several plants, thousands of employees, modular products comprised of hundreds of individual component parts, and powerful customers, each needing something different. As I recall, he answered something like, "There are only four basic, internal operating concerns that I need to monitor—safety, delivery, [i.e., timeliness, reliability] quality, and cost. For each of these, operations are either on track, getting better, or getting worse. It is that simple." Those very basic, very simple, very important aspects of his business each had a key performance indicator (KPI) associated with it, enabling regular monitoring. Each KPI, in turn, had a handful of subsidiary metrics whose measured amounts signaled something akin to "acceptable, keep it up, and keep striving to get better" or "unacceptable, take action to alter what is being done." This manager was confident that if the four KPIs were on target, year-end goals would be met.

And that is the critical issue—how strongly and reliably does an organization's KPIs connect to the outcomes sought? My experience suggests organizations have evolved in this quest in three ways.

First, over the years, some organizations have become more expansive in the desired results they pursue and the customized KPIs they use. Think of the prominence of "balanced scorecard" initiatives and externally oriented ESG (environment, social, and governance) discussions contained in published corporate annual reports. Not too many years ago, ESG and its related KPIs were not monitored, let alone published for external audiences. Moreover, whether an organization calls its internal array of KPIs a balanced scorecard or not does not matter—a balanced scorecard is merely a multidimensional array of performance measures.

Second, many organizations translate organization-level KPIs into internal KPI dashboards that are detailed and cascaded down to various levels of managerial responsibility. These dashboards enable real-time monitoring and, just as importantly, a line of sight for lower levels of management to see their connection and contribution to an organization's overall macro goals.

Third, organizations appear to revise and fine-tune the measures they embrace as KPIs. Again, evidence of this in the corporate world is the growing number of companies that, in their financial annual reports to shareholders, provide non-GAAP[46] performance measures in addition to those required by the authorities. Those organizations have ascertained that certain alternative measures are better indicators of the performance goals they pursue.[47]

There is a danger lurking in the KPI arena, though! The adage is true: "What gets measured is what gets done." Thus, there is an onus on organizations to make sure the measures they adopt for assessing results are encouraging managers and their direct reports to engage in the actions the organization most wants and needs. Conscientious organizations engage in what I term *behavioral audits*. This task begins with the identification of the KPIs used to evaluate a manager (or a cohort of managers). Next, each KPI is broken down into its component parts. A simple example is a return-on-assets (ROA) measure that has both a profit component and an investment-in-assets component. To increase ROA, managers will be incented to, in part, lower assets. For a particular manager, the monetary amount tied up in inventories might constitute a large part of their asset responsibilities. Once the component parts of each KPI are delineated, the behavioral audit identifies the behaviors a manager is incented to take regarding each of those component parts to achieve a favorable outcome on that KPI. In our example, the manager will be incented to lower their investment in inventory. What behaviors might they pursue to accomplish that? It would be important to anticipate that they might purchase less costly items and/or simply let inventory levels decline. If the anticipated behaviors are not the ones the organization desires (e.g., less costly goods might lower the quality of items acquired, and reduced quantities might result in an unacceptable number of backorder messages to customers), the next part of the behavioral audit process is to consider modifying the measures, recalibrating targeted levels, and/or introducing mitigating policies/controls (e.g., setting certain specifications pertaining to quality and establishing stipulated minimum levels of inventory quantities to be on hand). Behavioral audits are an important anticipatory "what-if" step in designing a final performance management/measurement system.

REFLECT: *Give some thought to two aspects of your organization's KPIs. When was the last time they were modified? Has the organization changed? If so, might the KPIs need to change also? Why or why not? Second, to what extent have your organization's KPIs been subjected to a behavioral audit? Have you applied a behavioral audit to the KPIs you are subjected to and for the KPIs that are used to evaluate your direct reports? If not, why not? Are you aware of any threads of organizational discontent with the performance measures currently in place? If so, what is the substance of that discontent? Have alternatives been considered? If not, why not?*

_____
_____
_____
_____

IDENTIFY: *Pick one arena of KPIs—those you are subject to, those your sales manager must meet, or those used to evaluate your fundraisers. Perform a behavioral audit on those KPIs. In short, deconstruct each KPI into its component parts. Note what behavior each of those parts is likely to induce on a stand-alone basis. Are those behaviors desired and beneficial to the organization? Do those incentivized behaviors warrant minor, major, or no restrictions? What refinement(s) to how those component parts are measured or defined is warranted and/or what sort of mitigating control or policy is worth considering for the organization to best garner desired and effective behaviors?*

SHARE: *Present your behavioral audit to a small group of peers. What response did you get? Is there support for such a periodic assessment? If so, why? If not, why not? Did any organizational objectives or means surface in the discussion as lacking robustly appropriate measures for their assessment? (Remember, "What gets measured is what gets done.") If so, should additional or different measures be developed, and if so, what?*

EVALUATE: *A behavioral audit applied to an organization's KPIs is best done in an anticipatory, proactive way—before an array of KPIs is implemented and utilized for performance assessment. Scan the organization for such an opportunity. Is there a new organizational unit beginning operations? Is there a new managerial position being created? Is there a new organizational mandate or opportunity garnering attention and resources? Bring to those new beginnings the behavioral audit mindset and approach.*

How was your behavioral audit suggestion received? If well, proceed with enthusiasm and dedication. If not, why not, and what does that say about the following: (1) relative priorities; (2)

the desire and ability for clear communication of expectations to involved personnel; (3) the degrees of freedom afforded decision makers; and (4) the consensus (or lack thereof) on direction and desired outcomes? If any of these raised concerns, you can make a strong case that a behavioral audit would be timely and helpful.

_____
_____
_____
_____
_____

... ANOTHER CHAPTER 3 VIGNETTE ...

> **#16 Ask hard questions
> even when receiving good financial news.**

> ... *questions are the most important intellectual tool
> we have* ... [48]

> —NEIL POSTMAN,
> American educator and social critic

REPORTING FINANCIAL RESULTS to interested external constituencies is an important stewardship function performed by the management of both for-profit and not-for-profit organizations. For the latter, providing information pertaining to the sources and uses of funds, along with any restrictions placed on those funds by providers, is a basic financial reporting obligation. For the former, earnings (profits) are a key financial reporting focus. In both organizations, managers often publish expectations regarding a reporting period's projected financial results well in advance of the start of that reporting period.

For-profit organizations that consistently report final earnings in line with their earlier stated expectations are thought to be well-managed and predictable in their performance. But such earnings results that are also consistently trending upward year after year warrant some probing questions rather than the more typical, satisfying celebration of achieved performance. In turbulent, unpredictable, and not uniformly growing economic environments, it should be surprising when financial earnings do not reflect that same turbulence.

The US Securities and Exchange Commission (SEC) has a stated interest in "earnings management." In general, earnings management is when managers make financial reporting decisions with more of an eye to meeting already-published earnings expectations than faithfully mirroring the ups and downs of the organization's market. It is tempting for some managers to engage in earnings management because they know that owners do not want volatile, and therefore unpredictable, financial earnings from the companies they invest in. The unpredictability of earnings translates to owners having to accept more financial risk and expecting higher returns for taking on that added risk. Then, as expectations for greater returns rise amongst owners, the pressure on managers increases dramatically to deliver higher returns. If the organization does not deliver those results, owners will not be pleased and will look for alternative ownership investments, and the company's stock price will decline—not a pretty picture.

A divisional company president once showed me a multiyear graph of the division's earnings performance. That graph depicted a smooth, upward trending line that was impressive. I asked him if he was concerned about his direct reports making their targeted numbers via means other than sound sales and expense management. Moreover, I wondered if the culture was such that one of his direct reports would be hesitant to ever tell him that their product line or their territory was going to fall short of expectations. This president assured me that everything was accurate, free of accounting and sales shenanigans, and his divisional group was extremely ethical. I hope that was true and continues to be. As impressive as that graph was, and it was, it also depicted for me a mounting pressure cooker for that president's direct reports to *not* be the one responsible for breaking the historical trend with a commensurate temptation to "push the envelope" in unsound ways.

Similar pressures exist within organizations of all kinds that utilize budgets to allocate resources and monitor manager performance. Meeting budgets is generally perceived as a sign of successful management. I do believe that is a valid premise. But probing with tough questions is also warranted, not to signal distrust or accusation but rather to ascertain viability. There are several different kinds of queries that a manager might use. The art of using questions for discovery and building assurance is important and can include the following types of questions[49]:

- *Open questions*—how were positive results achieved during such a tough period of time?
- *Closed questions*—were there any changes in policies or practices this period that affected the measurement of performance?
- *Probing questions*—what were some of the challenges you faced this period, and how were they addressed?
- *Clarifying questions*—could you help me understand how these specific challenges were addressed?
- *Recall questions*—how did this period's results and challenges differ from two years ago when we also encountered some difficult circumstances?
- *Process questions*—to what extent are the other unit managers facing similar circumstances, and how are they addressing those situations?

The litmus test for the answers you receive will always involve two further questions:

1. Do the financial results presented mirror what I know to be the reality of the events and circumstances?
2. Do I understand the explanation(s) given for the financial results? Could I effectively provide explanations to my boss, answering questions asked about them?

If the answer to either of these final two questions is no, there is more probing to pursue.[50]

REFLECT: *Good financial results are generally celebrated and rewarded. In your opinion and organization, are good financial results subjected to the same level and type of scrutiny as bad, disappointing results? Might a management team's stewardship responsibilities and due diligence commitments strongly suggest that the answer to that question must be "yes"? If not, why not? Do you ask hard questions about your direct reports' financial results when the results are good? If not, why not? If so, what types of questions do you ask, and are you satisfied?*

There is a lot to be learned from reading the accounts of some spectacular organizational financial failures presented in the SEC's findings and enforcement actions. Do you periodically inform yourself along those lines, and if not, why not?

If your organization has an internal audit staff and/or periodic external auditor review, meet with them to learn their observations and the nature and extent of any concerns they might have.

What kinds of pressures are your direct reports under, and what are the vulnerable aspects of financial results they are responsible for? Do you believe your direct reports feel that they can bring you bad financial news? Why or why not?

_____
_____
_____
_____

IDENTIFY: *Consider improving or enhancing your probing of good financial results for the organization as a whole and for your direct reports. Identify the foci for your questions. In what* *way(s) can your questions increase assurances of propriety and signal the importance of viable, ethical measurements, results, and practices? In what way(s) does that new line of questions also point to the need for some clear, a priori guidance? When was the last time a direct report brought you bad financial news? What transpired? Could you have handled that situation better? If so, in what specific way(s)?*

_____
_____
_____
_____

SHARE: *Might a concern for asking hard questions about good financial news warrant discussion in a management meeting? If so, ask for some agenda time without any accusations but with an appeal for due diligence and stewardship. Share stories from the press or the SEC archives. Yes, it can happen here too. Alternatively, if you think it better to share your thoughts with a trusted colleague or two, go that route to obtain reactions and suggestions. At a minimum, commit to asking probing financial-results questions of your direct reports and peers in the future when financial results are good. If possible, raise the prospect of a more formalized review process of good financial results on par with when not-so-good financial results are received.*

_____
_____
_____
_____

EVALUATE: *Whenever you brought up the topic of hard questions for good financial results, were you met with something akin to "That's not necessary. We have ethical people and/or sound guidelines"? If so, it's fine to appreciate that view, but embrace it with a healthy concern for someone, sometime, in some part of the organization facing pressures that could lead to violations of core norms and appropriate practices. Are the hard questions you ask or want to ask worth continuing, refining, or both? Why or why not? If you were summoned to court or interviewed by the press in the face of financial misrepresentation, what questions would you want to be able to say you always asked of your personnel?*

_____
_____
_____
_____

... A FINAL CHAPTER 3 VIGNETTE ...

> **#17 *Resolve and value disagreements.***

*It's hard arguing with people
who are looking for martyrdom.*[51]

—Nelson DeMille,
author of numerous New York Times #1 bestselling novels

WITHIN ORGANIZATIONAL TASK forces, committees, and management teams, it is not uncommon for disagreements to arise amongst group members. Those disagreements might pertain to such issues as priorities, direction, resources, processes, schedules, or even personnel. All too often, such disagreements are resolved in one of two ways: either the boss decides, or a majority vote holds sway. There is, however, a better, more effective, and more beneficial way to address disagreements. The best way to proceed is via a root cause analysis. Just like when a string of Christmas tree lights doesn't work, the "fix" becomes finding the bulb that disrupts the performance of the others. When disagreement amongst managers exists, the "fix" is finding the underlying root cause for that disagreement.

Over the years, I have learned a lot from my colleague Ed Freeman, a noted organizational ethicist and strategy expert. Together, we wrote about three possibilities to address a disagreement. At the most fundamental level, a disagreement may exist simply because different parties are using different facts. Thus, the first step is to make sure everyone is in possession of the same facts and a similarly shared knowledge of the institutional history surrounding those facts.

If a disagreement persists once all parties have the same factual information, the disagreement may be a function of how each party has framed the information. How issues, opportunities, and problems are framed can determine the desirability, variety, and number of choices each person envisions and, in turn, is able to consider. A classic example in this regard is seeing actions to improve the quality of a product or service as mostly about increasing costs versus seeing expenditures for improved quality as increasing customer satisfaction. It is possible that at this juncture of disagreeing, all that can be accomplished is that the parties acknowledge and articulate the different framings informing each other's thinking—an important accomplishment nonetheless since it sets the stage for the third potential root cause probe.

The third and final root cause possibility—differences in focus—has its own three distinct possibilities. The first is that managers may disagree because they have differing stakeholders in the forefront of their priorities. Stakeholders are those parties who will be affected, directly or indirectly, by the decision the group will ultimately pursue. Possible stakeholders include owners, the management team, customers/clients, a supplier, an organization's volunteers, a certain segment of the organization's workforce, and perhaps even identifiable segments of the local community. When managers are experiencing disagreement amongst themselves, it is useful to take the time for each of them to explicitly note for the others whom they see as the affected stakeholders.

If the disagreement continues even after everyone agrees on the stakeholders affected, then the next root cause possibility embedded in the "focus" category might pertain to the harms and benefits that accrue to each stakeholder group resulting from the potential decision under debate. All decisions allocate harms and benefits across stakeholders. The easy decisions are the ones that allocate benefits to all stakeholders and those that allocate harm to all—no nuance, only clarity. The difficult decisions are the ones allocating a mix of harms and benefits across stakeholders. It is possible that you and I might agree on the facts, on the framing, and even on the stakeholders affected, but maybe I had not envisioned one aspect of the outcome that you see as a harm, and you may not have envisioned another outcome that I see as a benefit. Those differences in perceived harms and benefits need to be surfaced, shared, and discussed. If simply being made aware of a harm or a benefit previously unforeseen does not resolve a disagreement, the final root cause possibility pertains to the core values the decision-makers each utilize.

Core values are operationalized in decision-making by the relative weights ascribed to a stakeholder and to a harm or benefit. A utilitarian-weighting approach that a manager might employ simply strives to operationalize "the greatest good for the greatest number of people." An egalitarian-weighting preference would consider the possibility that there might be one harm to one stakeholder that trumps any of the benefits that the other stakeholders might experience. Another core value example might be that you subscribe to full disclosure of information whether asked for it or not, whereas another managerial colleague subscribes to truth-telling but only regarding what has been requested. Core values, as a potential and bottom-line root cause for a disagreement, can be critical, and their discussion must be facilitated with care and respect.

A decision-making disagreement is best resolved via this sequenced, three-fold root cause analysis. It starts with a concern for shared *facts*, progresses to explore differences in *framings*, and if the disagreement persists, progresses to the *focus* each manager employs in the establishment of their position. Within *focus*, it begins with uncovering who each manager perceives as the pertinent *stakeholders*, then the articulation of *harms and benefits* to each agreed-on stakeholder, and if the disagreement persists, ends with an important discussion about the *core values* each manager uses to assess those harms and benefits to those stakeholders.

There are several potential benefits that can spring from such a conscientious approach to resolving disagreements. This process is likely to lead to:

- managers becoming more fully informed and savvy about each other's mindsets,
- managers becoming a more closely knit group,
- more innovative solutions arising for consideration,
- every member of the decision-making team becoming more fully engaged and lending their voice to future discussions and decisions,
- an increasing clarity of organizational mission and values,
- the management team acquiring confidence to receive subsequent criticism, and
- an under-debated or mis-debated discussion that would have led to a bad decision being implemented and/or to an omission of important "guardrails."

Managers are wise to probe disagreements when they arise through a specific process like that posed here to extract the potential value resident in the exploration of disagreement.[52]

REFLECT: *Recall a time when a significant disagreement arose amongst or between management colleagues. How was that disagreement addressed and resolved? Were that approach and outcome satisfactory in your mind? Why or why not? Did they lead to any sort of value-added insights or understanding? Think about when you have had a disagreement with direct reports. How did you handle that? In hindsight, was that approach satisfactory, positive, and value-added? If yes, in what way(s)? If not, why not?*

_____
_____
_____
_____

IDENTIFY: *Using at least one of the disagreements you reflected on above, subject it to the general approach for resolution presented here.*

- *Were all the facts present and available to all?*
- *How did the people involved frame the issue that gave rise to the disagreement?*
- *Who were the stakeholders most likely to be affected?*
- *What harms and benefits can you see as accruing to each stakeholder as a function of the disagreement being resolved in the proposed way and in the alternatively suggested way?*
- *What core values are germane to the evaluation of those harms and benefits?*

_____
_____
_____
_____

SHARE: *Share with a colleague the approach to addressing disagreements that you just fleshed out. Explain how it is intended to facilitate a search for the underlying root cause. Disagreement pertaining to a proposed decision is a manifestation of an underlying factor in need of discovery and discussion. Garner their reactions to, and suggestions for, the next steps you might consider for bringing this approach to a wider array of managerial colleagues.*

_____
_____
_____
_____

EVALUATE: *Are you encouraged to bring this approach to your colleagues? Why or why not? If so, start with a few. What were their reactions? Were you able to depict its usefulness through real examples and stories? Did the discussions spark insights? Did it prompt delving deeper into root cause? Did it surface important discussions? Did it lead to a better, more robust decision? If yes, consider a more extensive rollout of the approach for your organization or unit. If not, why not, and what adjustments might be warranted to continue with it?*

_____
_____
_____
_____

• • •

CHAPTER 4
Halftime. How Are You Doing?

Honesty: the best of all the lost arts.[53]

—Mark Twain,
author and American humorist

AS COACHES AND players in soccer, football, and basketball know, halftime is an opportunity to catch your breath, adjust, and recommit. At this juncture in your reading of this book, it is likely that you are either feeling frustrated and disappointed or pleased and excited to continue. Developing some of the important and challenging aspects of your MQ*p* is not necessarily an easy task. Some developmental paths may not come naturally, or they may require the relinquishing of long-held habits. In other instances, there is value in simply being reminded of the importance of a certain path, accompanied by encouragement and a bit of insight to do so. In whichever state you find yourself, honesty with yourself is important.

Here are some MQ*p* developmental honesty questions to ask yourself:

- **Have you been focused and diligent in developing an idea (or ideas) to potentially pursue sparked by the preceding vignettes?** If yes, fantastic! If not, why not? Does the answer to this "why not" question prompt its own pertinent management development issue, such as addressing a mindset of skepticism, a low energy level, or a satisfaction with the status quo? You can be your own best diagnostician and prescriber of a suitable remedy. Suspend doubt for a time and commit to seeing possibilities. Adhering to an MQp status quo condition is regressive because your organization is moving forward, even if at only a modest pace.

- **Have there been external roadblocks to your intended pursuits? Such as . . .**
    - **Not "enough time."** As part of my job, I am required to be a productive writer. Fortunately, I love that aspect of my job. Early in my career, meetings of all kinds resulted in my calendar looking like Swiss cheese. I could find no significant blocks of time where I could concentrate on writing projects. The solution? I started putting "writing" on my calendar for a couple of half-days each week. When asked about possible meeting times that conflicted with those reserved half-days, I could honestly say that I had a calendar conflict. Similarly, I had a colleague who would occasionally be seen with his feet up on his desk, hands folded across his midsection, eyes intensely staring ahead. When asked if he was daydreaming or napping, his reply was "I'm doing what I am paid, in part, to do—think!" We both had to take the time, regardless of the modest forces that came against us to do so, to do what we felt was an important part of our jobs. Is there something you might need to do if lack of time is an issue?
    - **No trusted colleague to act as a sounding board for your tentative ideas?** A trusted colleague may not be one nearby, nor do they need to be a best friend. A trusted colleague is someone who is not your boss, will honor requests for confidentiality, will be kind

and frank with their advice/reactions, and enjoys the quest for and consideration of new ideas. Such a person may be in another department or location, may be younger or older than you, and may not even be in your organization, but they are well-respected for their accomplishments and wisdom. At different times throughout my career, my trusted colleagues were of all these types. The beauty of such far-flung possibilities is that they may become a close friend through this process.

- **An inability to come up with anything concrete** from the *Reflect* and/or *Identify* prompts provided? Going to the memory bank and finding not much to withdraw is not good. Memories are there, and it is often the right key that must be found to unlock them. That key is often a story that prompts the thread of a memory that can then be pulled and unraveled into a full-scale recollection. This book has presented stories to help in that regard. If not stories, the key can be the conscientious task of recalling a celebration, a pain, a place, a person, a thrill, an "I liked that feeling" moment, or an "I never laughed [or cried] so hard" moment. All it takes is a spark to unlock an array of related memories if you are willing to mentally camp there, letting your mind explore that previously traversed terrain. From those memories, it is then useful to ask, "What management implications surface pertaining to people, process, purpose, or performance?" For each of those specific memories of most interest to you, what concrete idea arises in the arena of a pertinent vignette's theme posed in this book that can be undertaken to improve and expand your management capability in that regard? Spend more time with your people? Ask better questions? Become a better listener? Let others take the lead? Encourage entrepreneurial initiatives from others more often and more sincerely? Become a better learner from mistakes—yours and others'? Be more open to suggestions? It is my belief that there are always nuggets of managerial gold latent in everything we have seen or experienced that can be refined and brought to bear in our managerial todays and tomorrows.

- **How about those successful, earnest efforts to craft, share, and implement an idea sparked by a rich, reflective insight?** What surprised, intrigued, or pleased you the most about whatever level of success occurred? Why? Is there something replicable in what you did for other personal management initiatives? If not, why not? Is there something to be addressed in that regard? Have others noted the successful aspects of the initiatives you have undertaken? If not, have you needlessly kept it confidential, quiet, private? If yes, what sort of reinforcement and encouragement have you received from others? In what specific ways have you been fueled to continue, to expand, to develop along the MQp dimensions presented herein?

- **Is there merit in revisiting some of the less-than-successful initiatives and/or the successful ones you have undertaken because you can refine or expand the idea?** Perhaps there is a new trusted colleague you would like to involve in the deliberative sharing step. Maybe the initiative required more time and effort than was initially available, and you can now devote a bit more to it. It might make sense to revisit any initiatives that you want to before moving on to the second half of this book. Ascertain, as best as you can, if your energy and enthusiasm at this point is for finishing something you started or embarking on something new.

- **Before moving on in this book, take some time to craft a robust set of notes pertaining to each of the seventeen items already teed up for you so far.** Think of this task as creating a learning journal that captures all the pertinent thoughts, insights, wishes, tangents, and to-dos that relate to it. Such notes will be very helpful should you choose to revisit ideas later.

- **From the successes that you have experienced so far from using this book, are there some that you are committed to making a permanent part of your management mindset and repertoire?** If no, why not? Be honest. Are any of those "no" reasons amenable to mitigation? If so, be on the lookout for the moment and the means for their mitigation. If there are some that you do want to carry forward in a purposeful way, how can you best be encouraged and reminded to do so? Do you need to speak some of the commitments publicly, asking for support and periodic, friendly reminders? Do you need to put something on your calendar to remind yourself? Do you need to partner with a colleague to jointly encourage and execute an agreed-on management development practice together? I encourage you to do it.

- **Do you see a difference in how you interact with others? With problems? With opportunities?** Celebrate and acknowledge any managerial growth you see in this regard.

As you get ready to embark on the rest of the journey offered in the ensuing pages, make sure you have the energy and enthusiasm to do so wholeheartedly and authentically. The absence of either will be a hindrance. If circumstances at work or home are such that your attentions will be diverted from this endeavor more than normal, consider postponing your continued MQp pursuit. If it is a good time to proceed, give some thought to finding or adding another trusted colleague for sharing and vetting ideas. Based on what you experienced by going through the first half of this book, give some thought to the pace at which you plan to pursue the second half. Is one management possibility a week the right pace, or would it be better for a robust completion of the **RISE** process to play out for you by tackling one every other week or once a month? Obviously, the goal is not speed; it is thoroughness and experiential learning. Resident in that intended experiential learning is also experiencing the importance of reflection as a manager, the fun of ideation, the blessing of shared involvement, and the satisfaction of success.

Two final thoughts. First, the **RISE** process is intended to be facilitative, not prescriptive. If there is a tweak to that process that you find helpful, do it. For example, a vignette provided may spark the remembrance of a related but not identical event in your career. That is great. The key is that reflection is a skill and a discipline; it is the art of remembrance to extract lessons, not to birth regrets. And we all learn best in the context of a context—that is, an experience, an observation, an emotion we possess.

Second, you might find some interesting coffee-room chatter or pre-meeting chitchat will arise if you simply mention to some of your colleagues what you are doing to foster your personal MQp development. They may become interested in a similar pursuit, and you can share your approach with them. They may authentically volunteer to be a trusted colleague for you during your journey. Both possibilities can be rewarding and exciting.

May you finish the next part of your managerial development journey strong. Let me encourage you to proceed fully engaged. "He was a half-hearted manager" is not a comment we want said or thought at our retirement farewell or memorial service. Rather, we might want something akin to what I saw in Charlotte, NC, on the grave of Ruth

Graham (wife of the internationally known Billy Graham, "Pastor to Presidents"): "End of Construction. Thank you for your patience." As managers, we are mostly a work in progress... trying to be better every day... getting a bit closer to completion and excellence all the time.

Another epitaph I have seen with my own eyes is that of Thomas Jefferson, a former citizen of the town where I live. He had many accomplishments. He was the third president of the United States, vice president of the United States, governor of Virginia, minister to France, secretary of state under George Washington, a path-breaking botanist, a well-studied linguist, a renowned architect, an indefatigable inventor, and the visionary sponsor of the Lewis and Clark expedition. He was also the author of his own epitaph. Despite his many and varied accomplishments, he wanted his gravestone to note only three. His gravestone reads, "Here was buried Thomas Jefferson, author of the Declaration of American Independence, of the statute of Virginia for religious freedom, and father of the University of Virginia." He chose just these three, and he instructed his survivors to add "not a word more." These three highlight a love for freedom, for ideas, and for learning. Our managerial journey can be about the same three—the spark of new ideas, the freedom to try them, and the lessons learned from doing and observing. With a moment's forethought, what do we want said about our managerial careers? Similar points as Mr. Jefferson chose? Is it possible? Of course, it is. Why not now? I encourage you to go for it.

CHAPTER 5
Ideas for Action: Proactive-Focused
[vignettes #18–#26]

> **#18 *See over the horizon.***

*You see without assistance from the eyes,
over distances beyond the visual horizon.*[54]

—CHARLES A. LINDBERGH,
American aviation pioneer

MANY YEARS AGO, standing on the rim of a vast canyon, the author of a highly praised book about the Old West mused that a ragged band of cowboys and misfits must have thought, after miles and miles of flat, mostly featureless landscape that "They had come to the boundary that separated the everyday from the extraordinary."[55] In our own lives, and in the lives of the organizations we work for and with, where is that line between the everyday and the extraordinary? Where does the routine morph into the exceptional? When does today turn into tomorrow?

I have heard senior-level organizational managers note that their organizations had been so focused on process, operations, and execution that they feared their direct report managers were not ready for what was possible, the extraordinary opportunities "just around the bend" or "just over the hill." Those senior managers talked about their direct-report managers who aspired to become prominent organizational leaders needing to become "more strategic in their thinking," able to "lift up their eyes," needing to "see over the horizon."

Such admonitions make perfect sense and *wow*, what a tall order! Let me offer three ways that I have seen successfully employed for developing and honing such a capability. First, and perhaps the most obvious path to pursue in this regard, is to develop and learn from close—really close—relationships with an organization's key customers and competitors. For me, an organization's key customers/clients are the big ones, the small ones that aim to become big, and the big ones sought but not currently served. Key competitors are the handful of other organizations that are most like you, operate in adjacent markets, and could easily step into your realm. There is so much publicly available information about organizations that it is simply remiss to not know a whole lot about key customers and competitors. Organizations issue press releases and post them on their websites, their executives give speeches often available online, the press (local, national, and international) reports on them, universities write case studies about them, and if they are public companies, the SEC has a vast number of disclosures from them.

Second, find a thought leader that can challenge you to think in different ways. Chic Thompson and Jeanne Liedtka are two that I know, respect, and have seen in action doing this.[56] Buy any or all their books. Hire them for a speech or workshop at your organization. Watch them on YouTube. You won't be sorry. Chic is a creativity expert, and he has the credentials to back it up. Jeanne is a well-known and well-respected advocate for design thinking. Both have experience with businesses, governmental agencies, and not-for-profit organizations. What they both do, in their own unique and provocative ways, is facilitate thinking differently. Their firsthand stories are engaging, provocative, and exemplary. It is not the exceptional personality that can learn to think differently and more creatively—it is you and me if we want to.

The third means for developing a capability to "see over the horizon" is to take advantage of those who do that for a living. One of the best at doing so that I have come across is the Institute for the Future (IFTF). I first became aware of this organization many years ago when a client asked me to invite the IFTF for a couple of sessions at an international, multiday executive conference. Their sessions were outstanding and well received. Their newsletters, podcasts, and speaker's bureau stimulate purposeful ways of thinking about the future—seeing over the horizon.

> "[The IFTF is] the world's oldest continuously running futures research and educational organization. [They] develop custom forecasts, maps, and futures learning experiences, including innovation and design workshops, foresight training, and immersive learning journeys. [They] also produce future-themed conferences that bring innovators, experts, and learners together"
>
> (Source: www.iftf.org).

Many managers I know are mostly focused on the now, the impending, the task needing completion, not so much next year or where the current is likely to take them. Seeing over the horizon is seeing beyond the boundaries of the status quo, opening the door that potentially leads from the everyday to the extraordinary.

REFLECT: *Think about how different the work world around you is today versus when you started. Think about that in the context of just your organization. List as many of those changes as you can. Did anyone in your organization see them coming?*

Did you? Why not? What would you have had to be attuned to to have anticipated those changes? Are you truly convinced that unforeseen change is coming to your organization, functional area, and role? If not, why not? If yes, think expansively. What sorts of changes might there be just over the horizon that pertain to you and your managerial role?

_____

_____

_____

_____

IDENTIFY: *What sort of reading and professional development would be beneficial to you to be ready for what you might not yet know is coming? With whom would it be good to have periodic "over the horizon" conversations? What other organizations might be harbingers of what is to come for your organization? Develop a plan for learning all you can about that organization. Detail some of the steps you can take today to tap into such facilitative means for seeing over the horizon.*

_____

_____

_____

_____

SHARE: *Who else in your organization has an espoused concern/interest for the organization's future? Meet them; get to know them as best as possible. Share with them your interest in developing the capability to anticipate what might be looming* *ahead for the organization. Engage in "what-if" discussions (e.g., what if we had to become more like Uber? Amazon? YouTube? Whole Foods? GoFundMe? Stitch Fix? Upwork? What if organizations like Bain and Co., Walmart, ExxonMobil, or Disney became one of your competitors or partners? How might your organization have to change in response?). Which "what-if" discussions most energized or intrigued you and why?*

_____
_____
_____
_____
_____

EVALUATE: *Have you become known in your organization (or functional area) for being an over-the-horizon thinking manager? Why or why not? Have you found a ready and reliable resource to stimulate your thoughts and efforts in that regard? If not, why not? Have you found "what-if" discussions energizing and contagious? If yes, how can you nurture them to continue to be that? If not, why not?*

_____
_____
_____
_____
_____

... ANOTHER CHAPTER 5 VIGNETTE ...

> **#19 *Prototype to accelerate the process.***

One way to cheat and gain aerodynamic lift [in a helicopter] is to increase forward airspeed.[57]

—William F. Sine,
Senior Master Sergeant (ret.), USAF Pararescue

SOMETIMES, ORGANIZATIONS SIMPLY need more speed and more lift. They need to seize an opportunity sooner or pursue something bigger (what Jim Collins has popularly called a BHAG [bee hag]—a big, hairy, audacious goal[58]). Even well-intentioned organizational managers can miss the mark on both accounts. Think of all the hours spent in meetings painstakingly fine-tuning the steps to be taken and the voices to be heard in pursuing a new product/service/ outreach venture, an improved process initiative, or in drafting a final committee report or new grant proposal. Managers are sometimes guilty of equating more meetings and more discussions with progress. Tendencies to plan, discuss, study, debate, and review often turn into a second or third round of meetings to plan, discuss, study, debate, and review. There is nothing more deflating than becoming energized for the start of a new undertaking and slowly having that excitement and energy diffused through seemingly endless meetings and the droning on and on of all the mostly well-intentioned players. What is often beneficial in interrupting such deflating tendencies and in preserving and even creating more excitement and energy is fast prototyping.

A few years back, I had the opportunity to co-consult for a former vice chair of learning and education at an international professional services firm. A colleague and I had the responsibility of designing, developing, and delivering multiple high-profile professional development programs for the partners of that firm. The vice chair was the firm's sponsor for the endeavor, and her oft-used approach was to have a single, all-day meeting with us and the rest of her team to discuss the general specs, objectives, and audiences for that year's intended programs. She would then ask my colleague and me to come back to her in a couple of weeks with preliminary program designs. The designs were to include enough detail so that a decision could be made to proceed or not with each program as it was generally being proposed. Often, within the span of one subsequent meeting, through the process of our presenting and explaining the initial designs—and with her and her team probing, pushing, posing questions, and providing alternative/additional ideas—we had the final inputs necessary to revise the program designs one final time.

At first, it was frustrating to have our initial, carefully crafted designs dissected, questioned, and not accepted. What became apparent, though, was that it was her desire to fuel the creative, lets-get-concrete-about-the-details process underway and the inclusive gathering of others' ideas through a focus on those initial prototypes. It was my observation that she was opposed to trying to generate *all* pertinent inputs in an *a priori* planning vacuum without prototypes to spark reactions, fuel insights, and highlight agreed-on final details. In essence, the cycle time from the initial program discussion to the final design was shortened via this fast prototyping.

So, yes, plan and meet to an extent. Plan and meet to the point where an image has just begun to take shape in your mind's eye of an anticipated deliverable, and it is somewhat uncomfortable to stop meeting. Then, give a few talented people the challenge of building a prototype of the desired new product, service model, committee report, task force recommendations, or departmental initiative to fuel the next and potentially final meeting.[59] Prototypes foster shared bases for reactions and visualizations, and they facilitate seeing the omissions, holes, important connections, and weak spots in the ingredients required for completion. Chances are, there will be fewer overall hours spent in meetings with a fast-prototyping approach, and the hours that are spent in meetings will be more value-creating.

REFLECT: *"Good enough" has gotten a bad rap. For turbocharging or busting a stalemated or an about-to-be-derailed decision-making discussion, "good enough" can be a useful construct to galvanize the next steps. What recent or current opportunity-seizing, decision-making discussions have you participated in that seemed to get bogged down? Why did it get slowed or sidetracked? At that point, were there some preliminary decisions the group had already made? If so, was there a prototyping opportunity at that juncture for perhaps a (1) preliminary draft document, (2) rudimentary product mockup, (3) tentative flowchart of a possible streamlined process, or (4) partial simulation of a proposed new service experience/protocol? Think visually. What visual stimuli or cues, at that stalemated juncture, might have helped speed up the deliberations or stimulated participants to think more expansively?*

_____

_____

_____

_____

IDENTIFY: *For the next couple of weeks or months, commit to being a positive decision-making group discussion accelerant. Be sensitive to those points when group discussions have slowed, energy is in danger of draining, and something needs to be done* to maintain momentum and bolster enthusiasm. Look for those moments when shared visualizations can either bridge disparate viewpoints or provide a reasonable focus for discussing the specifics to continue the progress needed/wanted. *What prototyping ideas do you see as potentially helpful? What would it take for you to take the initiative to introduce those means at the appropriate time to either shorten or improve an extended decision-making process?*

_____
_____
_____
_____

SHARE: *Before introducing any such means into the decision-making deliberations, a reality check on two fronts might be warranted. First, ask a colleague if they sense the decision-making process having slowed or bogged down. If they agree, share with them your prototyping idea for getting things moving a bit faster or more constructively and ask for their opinion as to its appropriateness and likely effectiveness. In the end, if you believe your idea can help, not harm the process, take the initiative and see what happens.*

_____
_____
_____
_____

EVALUATE: *How did it go? Was your mid-process prototyping initiative useful in furthering, speeding, and deepening the decision-making discussions? If so, in what way(s)? If not, why* *not? Did you pick the right point in time to introduce it to the group, and what was key to getting that timing correct? Did the prototyping deliverable resonate well with your colleagues, and if so, why, and if not, why not? Were there any unintended positive or negative effects of your introduction of a visualizing prototype, and if so, what were they, and why did they surface? What might those insights portend for such future initiatives?*

_____
_____
_____
_____
_____

... ANOTHER CHAPTER 5 VIGNETTE ...

> **#20 *LBM—Let go. Back off. Move over.***

*There is an inverse relationship between
trust and micro-management.*[60]

—THOMAS RICKS,
winner of Pulitzer Prize for National Reporting

A BOARD MEMBER for several *Fortune* 500 companies once told me, "There is always ample glory and accolade to go around for every success." Think about that for a moment. Do you share the credit with your direct reports? Do you give them opportunities to shine? The elegance and appeal of such a simple view is that it preempts any natural tendency to worry about "my due" or "my recognitions." Because there is enough to go around, just like an incoming tide on which all boats rise, all involved can share in the glow of success. Great manager-mentors do not view accolades, rewards, and praise as zero-sum (that is, if you get a lot, then I get only a little). They never fear not getting credit. On the contrary, if I, as your manager, let go, back off, move over, and let you shine, we can both experience success. One of the toughest challenges newly appointed managers, and even many seasoned managers, face is letting direct reports function without intrusive interference or burdensome oversight. That is the way for great manager-mentors to effectively develop the next generation of managers.

I heard a similar message from a senior consultant who was on the receiving end of this management practice. As a young staff professional, she and a highly regarded manager were at a client's office. Ahead of time, they had decided that she would make the presentation, and the manager would simply be there for support. Great! Many managers might follow suit. One-third of the way into her presentation, the manager got up and left the room. Wow! Not many managers would have done that. She felt a moment of nervousness, but she knew her material well and proceeded. After the meeting, she asked her manager why he had left. He in essence replied, "You were doing great. I knew you were well prepared, and I knew you could handle the situation. Moreover, I also knew that if I stayed in the room, I would add my two cents' worth, and the client would focus on me. The best way I could think of to allow you to do what you were totally capable of doing was to leave." As she recounted that story, some twenty years later, she did so with deep respect for that seasoned manager. He had let go; he knew when to back off and move over. He knew that it was what she deserved and what would build her confidence and credibility. He also knew that the success of her presentation would benefit not only her but also their firm.

I had a similar experience. Early in my academic career, I was chair of my college's academic standards committee. Such an appointment, at such a vulnerable time in my career, was a signal that the school's administration had confidence in me. One year, the child of a high-profile personality was dismissed from school for failing to meet our academic standards. As you might surmise, I got a phone call from an irate parent demanding the child's reinstatement and asking, in not-so-polite terms, if I was fully aware of whom I was speaking to. Over the course of a five-minute rant, the caller informed me that the dean of the college, my boss, would hear about this. After the phone call ended, I headed to the dean's office to give him a heads-up. He calmly asked for a summary of the situation and the process the committee had used and then stated that I had his full support. What a huge confidence-builder. He did not intervene. He did not take control. He stood behind, in support of, me and the committee. I took his actions, or the lack thereof, as affirmation that he saw that I had what it took to be a full-fledged, valued member of the organization's cadre of professionals.

Such moments are priceless to those who are striving to succeed to make a mark. As a manager of others, you can gain a great deal from seizing opportunities to let go, back off, and move over. "After all," noted a high-ranking career US Coast Guard officer rather coyly but truthfully, "you get to be in the picture either way!"[61]

REFLECT: *Be honest: Do you desire the spotlight? Deep down, do you tend to take control of situations? Is there any part of your approach to managing that adheres to the adage, "If I want it done right, I have to do it myself"? Can you recall a time during your career when you were given a new, big, unexpected responsibility and left alone—in a trust-inspired, confidence-conveying way—to do it? If so, how did that feel? If not, would you have liked such an experience? If so, why?*

_____
_____
_____
_____

IDENTIFY: *Glance over the next week or month on your calendar. Identify a presentation or briefing you are slated to make. Is there an upcoming meeting you would normally lead or have a major role in? Who among the organization's talented younger generation could you delegate that task to? Is there a bright, generally reserved but very competent person who might not otherwise come to mind or be noticed during the normal busyness of the week who might welcome or benefit from receiving* *such a delegated role?*

SHARE: *Take a risk. With an appropriate amount of lead time for the task, meet face-to-face with the person you want to give a front-and-center opportunity to. Don't overplay the scenario by stating things such as "This is really important," "This is a career-builder," or "Here's a shot to stand out." Just note that you'd like that colleague to do this, that you have confidence that they can, and that you are available ahead of time should they have questions. Then, set that person free to fly. No fanfare. No trumpets. No organizational announcement. Just quiet, strong, conveyed assurance to the individual that you believe they can do it and can do it well. When the event starts, announce who will be taking the lead and then leave.*

EVALUATE: *After the event, reflect on how you felt leading up to it and as it took place. Did you have to resist a strong urge to stay, to jump in, to take the reins? Why? Why not? Chances are, the individual did not do it just as you would have, and yet there were bound to be some effective aspects to what they did—perhaps even some that hadn't occurred to you. Are you comfortable with* *acknowledging that? Why or why not? Are you comfortable with things being done differently from how you would have done them? Why or why not? What is the feedback from those in attendance? What lessons are embedded in that feedback for you and for your colleague? Is there a part of that person's confidence or sense of contribution or accomplishment that you see blossoming because of this experience? Identify ways to nurture that in them and look for similar opportunities to galvanize it in others.*

_____
_____
_____
_____

... ANOTHER CHAPTER 5 VIGNETTE ...

> **#21 *A little TPM goes a long way.***

> *... nobody wants to do maintenance.*[62]
>
> —Kurt Vonnegut,
> American author of novels, plays, and short stories

MAYBE YOU ONCE dreamed of being a pilot, speeding into a sunrise over the snowcaps of majestic mountains. I certainly had that siren call for a time in my younger days. Alas, my airline seats are in the economy-class section, not the cockpit. But I have frequently had the privilege of working with managers of corporate flight departments. This is generally a very impressive group of people. These managers have relentlessly pursued the concepts of outstanding customer service, zero operational defects, precise scheduling, and total safety long before most other organizational managers even began worrying about total quality management. Indeed, major corporate flight departments have a tenacious, proactive commitment to aircraft maintenance as part of an uncompromisable goal of delivering safe, comfortable, reliable, as-near-perfect-as-is-humanly-possible air transportation for their passengers. An entire flight department's personnel is attuned to this commitment and is sensitized to watch for anything that might undermine it. The approach taken to maintenance is planned, anticipatory, and meticulous. Perhaps more so than in a typical manufacturing plant or back-office operation, the stakes for a flight department are serious (i.e., life and death if landings do not equal takeoffs). Flight departments, along with nuclear power plants and hospitals, are a great example of what has been termed an HRO—a high-reliability organization.[63] These are organizations that must deliver their services with one-hundred-percent reliability and safety. Maintenance, vigilance, and training are key elements of an HRO.

On the maintenance front, and without calling such a concern for preventive maintenance anything fancy or catchy, corporate flight departments are engaged in what manufacturing circles popularly refer to as total productive maintenance (TPM). TPM is a proactive approach to equipment maintenance that seeks to preempt the root causes of breakdowns. It brings to bear a comprehensive consideration of maintenance methods and schedules, production priorities and demands, equipment complexities and capacities, as well as workflow and forecasts. Today, we see TPM successfully introduced and integrated into a growing number of manufacturing facilities (e.g., Alcoa Corporation).[64] I have also observed a TPM mindset active in nonmanufacturing settings such as customer/client follow-up, information technology installation, and all sorts of compliance settings. As customer demands for quality goods/services escalate, as costs of additional resources rise, as the losses due to rework and missed opportunities also rise, and as a desire for both effective and efficient processes increase the interdependencies of the resources at hand, the need for proactively maintaining the capabilities of not just equipment but also that of frontline managerial talent, information systems, and decision-making protocols has also risen. Oh, yes, fix it before it is broken—maintain and upgrade before it is necessary.

REFLECT: *What organizational talents, resources, or processes are you most reliant on? Why are you so reliant in that regard? Is there a bit of "we [I] take it for granted that it will continue to function the way it always has or the way we [I] need it to"? If so, what explains that reliance and outlook? Are* *you comfortable with that explanation? Why or why not? Who is responsible for maintaining the needed reliability and quality of that talent, resource, or process? Is there a regular check-in and checkup regarding those talents, resources, or processes? If not, why not?*

_____

_____

_____

_____

IDENTIFY: *What one or two ideas would serve to increase your confidence regarding the reliability and quality of the talents, resources, or processes you are most dependent on? Might those ideas prompt pertinent, regular assessment meetings? Proactively establishing scheduled training, updates, or overhauls? Improved personnel training and awareness? Creating a means for capturing and codifying user complaints or suggestions for improvement? In addition, a catalyst for new and good ideas can come from learning what other organizations have done. Why not plan a field visit to an HRO to observe their proactive approaches to talent, resource, or process maintenance and quality (or do some extensive reading in that regard)?*

_____

_____

_____

_____

SHARE: *A concern for and maintenance of personnel talents, reliably functioning equipment, machinery, and facilities,* *major operational and administrative processes, and IT is part of every manager's organizational stewardship responsibility. Find a colleague whom you believe has a keen interest in such a responsibility. Share with that person your idea(s) for implementing or improving the organization's TPM mindset, applicable to any part of the organization (it need not be restricted to only manufacturing-related assets). Does your colleague see the same need/opportunity? If so, why not? If not, does your colleague have a potentially more impactful idea that you can get excited about to jointly pursue? If they do like your idea, or you have agreed with their alternative, ask for a collaborative push to make it a reality sooner rather than later.*

_____
_____
_____
_____

EVALUATE: *How did the initiative work out? Is there now a marked improvement and/or increased confidence in the reliability and quality of the talent, resource, or process that you are most dependent on? Was it an uphill battle to get other managers to do their part in adopting the initiative you championed? If so, what mindsets or organizational hindrances might need to be addressed so that an HRO mindset is consistent and ongoing and that TPM plays a central role in that mindset for your organization or unit?*

_____
_____
_____
_____

... ANOTHER CHAPTER 5 VIGNETTE ...

> *#22 Look for opportunities to develop a "better mousetrap."*

If you build a better mousetrap, you will catch better mice.[65]

—GEORGE GOBEL,
an iconic twentieth-century American comedian

WE ARE LIVING amid a high-tech, convenience-valued, customer-facing, create-an-experience marketplace. Just think about how some everyday items and services have evolved over the recent past to become more effective, easier to use, widely available, and/or more indispensable. Examples are below.

- Going to a new friend's crosstown house once involved getting verbal directions from that friend. That means then gave way to a route designated on a hard copy, detailed, local map. Then, "I'll find it on MapQuest and print the directions" became an option, and that widely used resource has now mostly given way to GPS on our phones and in our car dashboards. It is still just getting directions, but GPS is so handy and easy. Perhaps the next better version of "getting directions" is cars with total autopilot and navigation to any desired destination we speak.

- Doing a school report once involved going to the public library to use its heavy, voluminous encyclopedias. That gave way to affordable home ownership of a set of hard copy encyclopedias, volumes 1 through 28. That then gave way to a modestly priced, complete encyclopedia on a computer disk. That approach has now given way to simply doing an internet search on a laptop at the kitchen table. It is still the assembling of pertinent information, but it is so much easier and more expansive. Perhaps the next better version of writing a school report is using artificial intelligence (AI) to write it for you or buying a completed report on any topic online. Oops, that option already exists.

- Not too long ago, a morning cup of hot coffee at home involved grinding the beans and putting them in a pot of hot water to simmer. That gave way to placing purchased ground coffee beans in a percolator pot. That gave way to countertop drip coffee makers. Then, the Keurig-type single-serving apparatus became popular. Now I have a machine that stores water and whole beans, and you press buttons for the water to heat and the beans to be ground. You choose the size of the serving, and it will heat up and foam the milk you want added. It is still just coffee, but it is much better. Perhaps the next better version of getting a cup of coffee is a coffee machine in a car's center console so there is no need to stop for one on the way to work or bring one from home.

- If you want music in your car, radios used to be an option for purchase when buying a new car. Then came 8-track stereo sound systems, then cassette tapes, then compact discs, and now satellite-based services like Pandora, Spotify, and SiriusXM. It is still just music, but now the music selection is customizable, extensive, and without geographic reception constraints. Perhaps the next better version of music in the car is for it to be streamed to each passenger seat on different channels so different passengers can listen to the music of their choice through the car's system.

- I can remember my mom doing laundry in an electric washing machine that had a hand wringer on top of it. (Before you think it—I'm not that old. My parents were slow to replace what worked well and wasn't broken.) She would hand crank the wet clothes through the wringer, squeezing out most of the water. She had to hang the clothes outside on a long line to dry. Obviously, that morphed into washing machines with spin cycles to eliminate excess water and an electric dryer that dries clothes. If those appliances took up too much space, you could stack them, one on top of the other. Now, General Electric has a single appliance that washes and dries, eliminating the need for two appliances and the transfer of laundry from one to the other.

There are numerous examples like these. The product and service line extensions that I am always most intrigued with, however, are the ones that, when I see them, I say to myself, "That's ingenious. That's an example of the proverbial 'better mouse trap.'" Stylish untucked collared shirts→ UNTUCKit LLC shirts. Easy slip-on shoes with a built-in shoehorn→ Skechers USA, Inc. Economical home security→ doorbells enhanced with wireless video cameras.

Two more examples. I don't know anyone who does not enjoy sitting around a campfire on a cool, cloudless evening with the stars twinkling like diamonds draped across the front of a black dress. The crackling sounds of burning firewood and the dancing flames with hues of yellow, red, blue, and orange all please the senses. But then, your eyes begin to burn, and your clothes begin to smell as the swirling and blowing smoke ruins the ambiance. Solo Brands, Inc. to the rescue with a virtually smokeless firepit, an innovative design that takes full advantage of the principles of combustion and airflow that has truly brought the enjoyment back to a backyard firepit experience. I wish I had been able to solve that smoke problem and create an affordable firepit for backyard use. Perhaps a tabletop, personal version of the Solo Stove is the next good extension. Darn, it has already been thought of, crafted, and made available for sale.

A second example. Parents of newborn babies face a big problem—their own lack of uninterrupted sleep. In the absence of any relief, that sleep deficit accumulates and compounds until one or both parents are frazzled, fatigued, and sometimes functioning in a semicomatose state. Tempers flare more quickly. Focusing on job-related activities becomes more difficult. Home to-dos go undone. There are no beneficial effects from lack of restful sleep. And, in the middle of the night, when the baby begins crying, the remedy is usually rocking and/or feeding the little darling. As a first response, Newell Brands, Inc.'s Graco brand and Happiest Baby, Inc. have both developed a bassinet that steps into the breach of trying to rock the baby back to sleep. They have developed a sound-activated rocking bassinet. A baby begins crying, the bassinet registers the sound, and the gentle rocking of the bassinet begins. And, just as a parent would, if the crying gets a little louder, the bassinet rocks a bit more vigorously. Some models even turn on white noise to soothe the crying baby. The crying-triggered rocking and soothing sound features can provide parents with better odds for a bit more sleep. I wish I had thought of such a bassinet. Perhaps the next improvement to preserve parents' sleep with a crying baby is a bassinet with an auto bottle feeding station activated after a certain amount of crying, followed by an auto-inclined burping segment.

One more example. When I was a college student several decades ago, I remember a professor going on a riff about new product ideas lodged in his mind simply based on things he wanted to improve in his life. One of the things he mentioned pertained to his new car. He wanted removable rubber trunk liners, so hauling dirty items would not be a problem. As far as I know, he did nothing with that idea. Well, maybe he did and is a silent investor/founder of WeatherTech Company that makes such liners—actually, I don't think he is. For him, it was a missed opportunity to develop and capitalize on a simple "better mousetrap" idea emanating from a curiosity for simple and effective improvements to everyday living. What are yours?

REFLECT: *Are you frequently giving thought to your organization's client/customer/donor experience and needs? Even if you do not work in marketing, product, or service line development, this can and should be a part of your managerial mindset. If it has not been, why not? (You have a customer/client/donor—if not an external one, an internal one.) Recollect any conversations or thoughts from the past that you had of the ilk: "If we did _____, we could lower costs or improve functionality or make our product or service more appealing." What would you insert in that blank, and why? Feel free to come up with more than one possibility.*

_____

_____

_____

_____

IDENTIFY: *What did you select to fill in the blank place above? "If we did _____, we could . . ." Return to that thought. Refine it. Test it against the goal of an improved outcome for a client, customer, donor, or another constituent. Does it lower the price? Does it improve functionality? Does it extend usage? Does it improve service? Does it become more competitively appealing? Does it meet an evolving or emergent need? Does it do one or more of these? Is it feasible to do?*

_____

_____

_____

_____

SHARE: *Vet your idea by asking a couple of friends questions: Would this new product/service appeal to you? If yes, why? If not, why not? If yes, what do you like best? Does this meet a need that you have? Might it lead to increased brand loyalty? What sort of word-of-mouth or social media recommendations would they make for it? How would you pitch it, and to whom?*

_____
_____
_____
_____

EVALUATE: *Assess the reactions you got from sharing your idea. In general, is there excitement to move ahead? If not, why not, and could those hesitations be mitigated? What sort of approval do you need to obtain to move ahead? Are you confident enough to seek that? If not, why not? What sort of collaboration do you need, and can you obtain that? If not, why not? Bottom line: What benefit(s) do you envision accruing to customers/clients/donors and to the organization? Are those worth pursuing with passion and energy? If yes, why not give it a try using fast prototyping (see #19) as an appropriate approach to pursue?*

_____
_____
_____
_____

... ANOTHER CHAPTER 5 VIGNETTE ...

> *#23 New product ideas can emerge from anyone, anywhere, at any time.*

Heroes aren't designated in advance.[66]

—Marcus Luttrell,
former US Navy Seal and author of
New York Times bestseller *Lone Survivor*

HERE'S A QUICK quiz. What pairings between the two columns below led to a new product, process, or partnership idea?

1. Failed adhesive	A. Toyota car plant
2. Oncology surgeon	B. Snack food manufacturer
3. Goat rancher	C. College frat party
4. NASCAR	D. Church choir
5. Wet leaves	E. Hospital ER
6. Bicycle foot pump	F. Utility rights-of-way

The answers might surprise you (continue reading). Did you get any right? If not, can you envision the possibilities arising from some of the pairings? If you answered yes to either question, you have a creative spark, a spark waiting to be fanned into a full-blown flame. This spark may have surfaced despite long-held thoughts about yourself not being creative. It is true: most of us have too easily relinquished youthful abandon that was always eager to consider and pursue novel possibilities.

Remember that out-of-the-box idea you suggested to the boss a few years back and the look you got? How about those times you saw an innovation roll through the company, and you thought, *What's so earth-shaking about that? I could have come up with that. Why didn't I?* Many of us sent any self-image of "I'm creative" packing long ago. We have filled the void with substitute thoughts of *I'm a hard worker, I'm a good motivator of people, No one can run the numbers like I can*, or *I can sell ice to Arctic residents*. Indeed, these traits probably were our ticket into the managerial ranks of the organizations where we work.

But creativity may not be what we think it is. Maybe creative people don't always fit our stereotype. Maybe creativity is not about being artistic, off-the-wall, having patentable ideas coursing through our psyche a mile a minute, or even being someone who periodically daydreams about realities unseen but hoped for. Maybe you really are creative.

According to Thomas Disch, a renowned American science fiction writer, "Creativeness is the ability to see relationships where none exist."[67] Steve Jobs, of Apple Inc., agrees: "Creativity is just connecting things . . . creative people . . . [are] able to connect experiences they've had and synthesize new things."[68] Wow, that changes things. We don't have to think of creativity as exclusively an endowed trait some people (that person over there) are born with and others (yourself) are not. We can be creative by exploring the juxtapositions of disparate things we observe in our surroundings. We can learn to explore and even play with those combinations to spark different possibilities for improving an organizational process, developing a new product, implementing a new service, or launching an expansive and powerful partnership. Here are the stories behind the answers to the preceding quiz, each epitomizing the connection of the seemingly unconnectable.

Failed Adhesive + Church Choir = 3M Company's Post-it Notes Product Line

Maybe you have heard this popular story. A 3M researcher was exploring ways to create a super-strong adhesive; instead, he found a low adhesive that would stick to things but not adhere. He showed it to some of his colleagues, but no one really knew what to do with it until one came up with an application when singing in a church choir. Doing what? Where? That's right. Singing in a church choir. This singing engineer was tired of the bookmarks that would not stay in the sheet music. He applied this weak adhesive to his bookmarks and found that they stayed in place and could be easily removed and reused. Bingo! Decades later, 3M Company's Post-it Notes are still going strong and have even entered our everyday lexicon.[69]

Oncology Surgeon + Toyota Car Plant = Patient-Monitored Surgical Recovery Protocol

A revered surgeon and his colleagues at the medical center were asked to attend what seemed like "yet another" professional development seminar. This time, however, it was given by a business school, folks who did not know much about medicine other than receiving it. It was the Toyota Motor Corporation production case study that really caught his attention. Part of Toyota's manufacturing program involved a stipulated set of production quality indicators. Any production worker could stop the assembly line if they saw something in violation of those indicators. A thought crystallized in his mind. He could develop a similar set of indicators applicable to a patient's postsurgical recovery progress and give it not to the medical team but to the patient and the patient's family. That way, patients would know the markers to look for on each subsequent day after surgery and ascertain whether they were on track. If certain things were not happening according to the indicators, they could let the medical staff know, and the caregivers could factor those additional observations into their patient plan. His short, easily read, and understood quality-of-recovery document was simple and robust, and it works. My family benefited from using it.

Goat Rancher + Utility Rights-of-Way = Goat Busters Brush Management Partnerships

What do you do with an entrepreneurial spirit, an environmental science degree, and a recession? Look for work wherever you can. A young university grad took a job with a landscape company in his hometown, not knowing what the future might hold. In due time, he learned of an ongoing, large-scale challenge faced by highway and utility right-of-way managers, commercial and residential land developers, farmers, neighborhood associations, and park managers. The challenge was to create sustainable, effective, affordable, environmentally friendly brush management, natural fire protection, and invasive vegetation control programs. Predisposed to making friends, he became friends with a goat rancher. True to their stereotype, he saw that goats eat just about anything—quickly. Without any fanfare, he and his goat rancher friend latched onto the idea that goats would be an environmentally friendly, low-cost, effective way to provide that long list of customers with the results they desired. How? They partnered with Goat Busters, an operation with portable fencing and goats to put in places to clear the unwanted vegetation. Ingenious.

NASCAR + Hospital ER = Improved ER Processes

Chic Thompson, a noted creativity guru, has led brainstorming sessions with organizations as diverse as Norfolk Southern Corporation, the Young Presidents' Organization, and NASA. I have heard him recount a story pertaining to a brainstorming session with personnel from various hospital emergency room departments on the general topic of improving speed, efficiency, teamwork, and excellence. An interesting idea surfaced in his mind. What might they learn from a NASCAR pit crew? Indeed, he has taken teams of hospital staff to NASCAR sites to observe those crews in action. Invariably, and as a result, hospital staff have generated ideas for streamlining their protocols, improving their teamwork, speeding up their diagnoses, and/or reducing mistakes.

Wet Leaves + Snack Food Manufacturer = PRINGLES Potato Chip Product Line

Consider Procter & Gamble Company's Pringles potato chips—those chips stacked in a tennis-ball-like canister. Who would have ever thought of stacking potato chips, that wonderfully salty snack that generally comes in a bag and, like snowflakes, possesses a variety of distinct shapes, sizes, curls, and dimensions? Well, someone observed that wet leaves could be conformed to a layered, nested, stacked configuration.[70] So the company developed a wet-leaf-like production process, and a whole new product line was created.

Bicycle Foot Pump + Party Open Bar = Hands-Free Keg Tap Product Idea

College kids never lack ideas, ideals, and idiot pranks. As for the first of this youthful trinity, I happened to be at a Christmas party with more seasoned adults and a few of their college-aged offspring. Of course, the college kids were there for the free food, and their parties weren't due to ramp up until ours was winding down. In speaking with one of them, who hailed from Texas, I learned that he was all excited about a product idea he wanted to explore. He had conceived of a foot-operated, hands-free beer keg tap. His aha moment had come one day while using a foot pump to inflate his bicycle tires. A similar hands-free device would sure make filling beer cups from a tap a lot easier. In fact, you would be able to fill two or three at a time. As I harkened back to my college days, it sounded like a good idea. Perhaps he or someone else followed through on this idea with a marketable product and/or a patent.

Such stories simply underscore the fact that the origins of many new product and service ideas are not rocket science. Rather, they are often the creative juxtaposition of seemingly disparate things we already see, know, or use. Tune your thinking in that direction from time to time. You never know! Cultivate, nurture, and feed your flow of observational inputs, intentionally connecting them in creative and simple ways to see what ideas germinate.

REFLECT: *On a scale of 1 to 10 (10 being DaVinci and 1 being Dilbert), how creative do you think you are? If you ranked yourself lower than 5, why such a low rating? If slightly higher than 5, why not higher? Jot down several reasons why you discount your creative ability. Note the personal and institutional factors at play in that self-rating. Do you lack confidence, focus, motivation, and/or opportunity? What would it feel like to have a novel idea lauded by those you regularly interact with and respect? When was the last time you had that feeling?*

_____

_____

_____

IDENTIFY: *First, which of the following work-related contexts presents you with the most comfortable and best potential for applying your creative spark: Product/service innovation? Relationship management? Partnership affiliation? Process improvement? Culture building? Next, identify five items from,* *features of, or facts about what you like best about your living situation (e.g., remote control TV, early morning newspaper, timer on coffee pot, soft bed, proximity to good shopping). Or similarly, list five items from, features of, or facts about your regular recreational endeavors that you most enjoy (e.g., clear lake water, fast boats, a warm sleeping bag on a cool mountain night, laughter of friends and family on a riverfront dock, eating outdoors). Ruminate on and flesh out the appeal embedded in those highlights.*

_____
_____
_____
_____
_____

SHARE: *With a colleague or two, present your list with a brief explanation of what you are doing and how you got to that point. Then, note for them the work-related context you have chosen to focus on. Now make a pairing from your list (either the living situation list or the enjoyable recreation list) with the work-related context you selected. For example, "timer on coffee pot" is connected with a work context centered on the challenge colleges face of not wanting students to surf the web during class. What ideas arise (e.g., automatic timer system shut off or electronic blockage of students' access to the web during in-class hours)? Repeat using additional items from your list. For example, "lounging on the dock" coupled with the partnership affiliation-work context at my university might lead to ideas like the following: with a local landscape or pool company, create outdoor conversational areas on campus around small fishponds, or put soothing-sounding fountains in the library and/or student lounges in exchange for free advertising space. Keep your ideas flowing until your energy wanes.*

EVALUATE: *Identify one or two promising, energizing work-related ideas resulting from the "share" activity just completed. Note their positive workplace implications. Might others get excited by that potential? Who? Talk to them about your idea. Sketch out the beginnings of a plan to make your idea a reality. Does it look workable? If yes, begin. If not, why not? Can those reasons be overcome? Does the potential payoff of your idea exceed the hassle of addressing the hindrances? If so, go for it. If not, cycle back through the reflection, identify, and share steps to gravitate toward an idea that is doable.*

... ANOTHER CHAPTER 5 VIGNETTE ...

> **#24** *"Never too old to be wrong or too young to be right."*

... she was a couple years younger than I was and maybe a decade wiser.[71]

—JAMES PATTERSON,
bestselling author and recipient
of the US National Humanities Medal

IT IS A dramatic understatement to note that the work world has changed significantly during my career. Many of those changes are for the better and have been galvanized by amazing advances in technology and important societal changes. In many instances, the voice and energy for those changes have come from the workforce's younger generation. Informally and quite naturally, older members of the workforce have benefited from the reverse mentoring that younger colleagues have provided in the use and power of ever-evolving information technology. Perhaps that phenomenon started, or accelerated, the demise of a norm that had existed for years—young people must wait their turn and "pay their dues" while organizations are led and managed by the most experienced, older managers. As a friend of mine recently quipped to an audience of her direct reports, "You are never too old to be wrong or too young to be right."[72]

With a responsibility for hundreds of employees and billions of taxpayer dollars, she was acknowledging that she wanted good ideas—period. Moreover, just because someone is a junior member of a team does not mean their ideas should be dismissed or discounted. Similarly, an idea presented by the most senior person should not be assumed to be the best one to pursue. In essence, her teams were tasked with (1) generating ideas for improved organizational performance, (2) doing their due diligence regarding those ideas, and (3) constructively and critically evaluating the ideas that surfaced without deference to age, seniority, or title.

The famous stories of the founding of Apple Inc., Facebook (now a part of Meta Platforms, Inc.), and Microsoft Corporation by bright, young, forward-thinking entrepreneurs have been well-chronicled. On perhaps a less transformative and well-known basis, but with lots of upside, nonetheless, consider W&P Design, a Brooklyn-based company founded by two friends shortly after graduating from college. During college, Josh Williams and Eric Prum[73] catered local parties and enjoyed crafting and serving specialty cocktails. From such a simple setting, a simple idea was born based on an existing simple product. Williams and Prum converted the everyday, classic mason jar that I saw my grandmother use for canning fruits and vegetables into a hip cocktail shaker. They developed, used, produced, and sold their "Mason Shaker" and its accompanying "Mason Tap" (a screw-on pour spout). Major retailers began to carry the product. Hundreds of other sustainable and eco-friendly food- and beverage-related products have emerged from these humble beginnings of their design business. With gusto and class, they have coauthored two upscale cocktail books (*Infuse* and *Shake*). And their latest venture is Very Great Inc., which, according to the company's website (www.verygreat.nyc/), "is a digitally-native consumer product platform and holding company, growing a family of real, crave-worthy brands for a new generation. [It is] designed to rapidly develop, launch and scale modern consumer product brands." For these two, it all started with a mason jar in college when they were barely twenty.

Jeffrey Katzenberg of Walt Disney Company and DreamWorks SKG fame, along with Meg Whitman of eBay Inc. and Hewlett-Packard

Enterprise Company fame, have had a long and high-profile run as successful entrepreneurs and top corporate executives. Katzenberg and Whitman were instrumental in envisioning, launching, and leading Quibi, a company designed to be a streaming service for handheld devices. It would be "specializing in content built for quick consumption . . . TV episodes . . . less than 10 minutes and movies . . . broken down into chapters."[74] The company lasted only several months, and its investors lost money. Just like the truth spoken by investment advisors when they caution clients—"past performance is no guarantee of future performance"—the same should be considered applicable to the ideas emanating from even the most seasoned and senior organizational members.

All ideas are subject to scrutiny, due diligence, and thoughtful consideration. Just because someone has been around a long time, even with past success, does not mean their next idea is worth pursuing. Likewise, just because someone is young and new to the organization does not mean their idea is not worthy of serious consideration.

REFLECT: *If you are a relatively young and junior manager, have you recently felt that your idea or suggestion was ignored or discounted? If not, what was the key to being heard and valued? If yes, what effect did that have on you? In retrospect, would you now agree that a better idea or suggestion came from someone else? Be honest. Do you think you could have stated your idea or suggestion better—more clearly, more persuasively, more collaboratively? If you are a more seasoned manager, can you recall a time when your ideas felt ignored or discounted? Recall what that made you think and feel. Are you and/or your senior colleagues guilty of doing that toward your younger, junior colleagues? If so, why does that tend to happen?*

_____

_____

_____

IDENTIFY: *Reconstruct the details, as best you can, of a circumstance where a young junior manager's idea or suggestion was not adequately considered and discussed. Reconstruct the details, as best as you can, of the situation surrounding the ready acceptance, with minimal vetting and discussion, of an older, more senior manager's idea or suggestion. For either, or both, what specific things would you like to see change in how future deliberations and discussions of ideas and suggestions are handled? What would be beneficial for both the younger and older managers to do differently or better in this regard?*

_____

_____

_____

_____

SHARE: *Arrange for a meeting with three people: you, a managerial peer, and a younger or older colleague, depending on your relative seniority. Share with them your observations of younger voices being disregarded in contrast to the general acceptance of, with minimal discussion, the ideas and suggestions from older, more senior voices. Gently remind them that your observations, sincerely arrived at, are not the discussion point. Encourage a conversation that accepts your premise. Ask them what they may have observed and what ideas come to mind when mitigating this organizational concern. Then, share with them your ideas for how to do so. Be as concrete as possible, seeking their counsel as to any tweaks that might make your idea more effective* *and/or easier to implement. End the meeting with a request for their support and willingness to give your collaboratively tweaked idea a try in the ensuing weeks.*

EVALUATE: *In the wake of several weeks' normal meetings, formal or informal, give some thought to how your ideas for better acceptance of, or listening to, ideas from the younger members of the management ranks went. Similarly, give some thought to how your attempts to foster more open and frank discussions pertaining to the ideas and suggestions from more senior members went. Next, reconvene your small group for a meeting to learn what they saw, experienced, and have concluded. Share with them your conclusions. Finally, engage in a codifying discussion to see what ideas merit continued focus and perhaps refinement. Remember, the goal is for an organization to be more open to the possibility of good ideas emanating from its younger managers and the possibility that just because someone is more senior, their idea may not be the best.*

... ANOTHER CHAPTER 5 VIGNETTE ...

> #25 *Simple is in.*

The greatest ideas are the simplest.[75]

—Sir William Golding,
winner Nobel Prize for Literature

SIMPLE IS NOT the same as easy. Yet, savvy managers must doggedly pursue simple solutions, simple strategies, and reliably simple systems. At my home organization, then General Electric Company CEO Jeff Immelt visited and gave a speech to our student body. In that speech, he encouraged MBA students to make a name for themselves during their careers by transforming complex processes and strategies into simple ones.[76] Organizations need more effective simplicity because it is most sustainable, replicable, and less prone to failures.

It is worth repeating—simplicity is desirable, and it can work. Take, for example, the enormously successful fast-food chain Wendy's.[77] The Wendy's Company was not the first hamburger fast-food restaurant chain to appear on the scene, nor was it innovative in its food-preparation technology. Wendy's was, however, the first with a novel, simple marketing strategy that had tremendous customer appeal: "hot and juicy." Those simple adjectives defined their product, differentiating it from the "multimillion-sold" competition's precooked, resting-under-the-heat-lamp patties.

Wendy's goal was, and remains, to retain a fast order and delivery capability while providing customers with a burger right from the grill. To achieve fast service *and* "hot and juicy"—something no other competitor was doing—Wendy's had to anticipate customer demand throughout the day and begin cooking hamburgers in anticipation of upcoming customer traffic. I'm sure an immediate question arose from some thoughtful early insider: "We can't leave our overestimated, not-needed burgers on the grill indefinitely, and we can't serve customers overcooked burgers. Moreover, we aren't going to place rows of wrapped burgers under heat lamps as if we are incubating baby chicks. What do we do with those cooked patties that exceed customer demand?" The simple, elegantly innovative solution gave birth to a new product offering: chili. Indeed, one day's overproduced (note that I did not say "overcooked") hamburger patty production became the main component of the next day's chili batch.

Consider two more important questions. How does Wendy's convey the distinctive "hot and juicy" feature to customers? They do it by simply placing the grill where customers can see it, having no wrapped burgers under a heat lamp, and using a square hamburger patty whose corners and edges extend beyond the round bun so that it is clearly visible. How does Wendy's provide regular-size hamburgers and jumbo burgers without having to fine-tune a forecasting model to that level of refinement? They do it by only cooking single patties and "building" burgers with one, two, or three patties depending on a customer's order.

In the end, this comprehensive strategy—one with huge customer appeal—became operational with an elegantly simple and insightful product line extension. Without the chili concept, fast, "hot, and juicy" would have been too wasteful, and Wendy's would probably not have been able to differentiate itself quite so effectively from its competitors. Simplicity works.

Central Virginia-based Plow & Hearth LLC, the home and garden company, locates its retail outlet store next door to one of its regular retail stores. The company wants to sell its outlet merchandise, and as is true with outlets, quantities on hand vary over time. No problem, though. I am sure they are aware that, like many other customers, I always go to the outlet store first. If I find something I would like two or three of (e.g., deck chairs), I buy the one the outlet has at its greatly reduced price and then immediately go to the regular retail store next door to get the other two. This is a simple strategy to geographically colocate retail establishments where one, in many instances, generates customers for the other. (And I haven't even mentioned the cost savings from the two establishments sharing one parking lot and representing one stopping point for the company's trucks.) Simplicity works.

Another example of a simple but effective strategy is that used by many grocery stores with loyalty cards. These cards not only generate immediate discounts on some products; they also generate customized coupons for customers based on their purchases. Quite simply, the company's information system links a customer's purchasing behavior to an incentive to come back next week to buy similar or related things from them. Reasonable. Effective. Simple.

I can't help myself . . . I have one more example. In the late 1990s, a smart young man, during his MBA studies, revolutionized the loan industry with a simple concept—flip the tables. "After experiencing the frustrations and complexities of getting his first mortgage, Doug [Lebda] envisioned a way to simplify the loan shopping process. Instead of physically going to multiple banks, customers could go to a [single] website where the banks would compete for their business."[78] That simple change in focus led to his creation of LendingTree, Inc., which went public in 2000 and is still "empowering consumers and changing how people shop for financing."[79]

REFLECT: *Think about a significant process in your organization that frustrates you the most. Is it the budgeting* process? Product delivery process? Performance review process? Customer service process? Product inspection process? Purchasing process? Employee scheduling process? Expense reimbursement process? There is bound to be one or more in your organization. Why does it frustrate you? From a different angle, think of a frustrating or time-wasting experience you have recently had as a customer, resource requester, or service provider. What was it about that experience that was irritating? How might that recollection help inform your thinking about the organizational process you identified?

_____
_____
_____
_____
_____

IDENTIFY: *How might one or more of the above processes be enhanced via simplification? Simplification can serve to shorten the time frame, the number of steps, and/or the number of people involved. This week, pick one process and identify one way to shorten its time, reduce its steps, or avoid involving one person. Identify another process for the same scrutiny next week.*

_____
_____
_____
_____
_____

SHARE: *Explain your two simplification ideas to a colleague. Do they like them? Why or why not? What alternative or complementary idea do they suggest? Enlist this person and mutually* *agree on taking steps to implement a process simplification.*

EVALUATE: *An interesting aspect of this endeavor is to evaluate, after the fact, what sort of response/reaction you got from those people affected by your simplification initiative. Did they see the merits of your idea? Were they wedded to the old ways? Were they helpful? Did your initiative energize them to offer or undertake their own additional simplification steps? To all these questions, note why or why not. The answers are likely to reveal something key about the organization's culture, habits, and energy. Did your initiative truly result in a simplified process without loss of quality? If there are natural extensions springing from what you accomplished that should be pursued, contemplate how best to pursue them. Plan to remain vigilant regarding the original simplification you initiated so that it is preserved and/ or improved.*

. . . A FINAL CHAPTER 5 VIGNETTE. . .

> **#26 *Fundamentals matter. Codify yours.***

Get the fundamentals down and the level of everything you do will rise.[80]

—MICHAEL JORDAN,
Hall of Fame pro basketball player

EVERY YEAR, I am privileged to interact with hundreds of seasoned managers. The ideas, experiences, reflections, and concerns we share provide the grist for countless conversations that stimulate and stretch their learning as well as mine. Their daily successes occur on the front lines of their respective organizations generally without much fanfare. You will not hear them interviewed on cable news shows. You will not see their faces on book jackets. You will not meet them on the dais after a high-profile professional conference. Yet the unheralded lessons I have drawn from these managers represent a baker's dozen of management fundamentals to always keep in mind. These are not fads. They are enduring principles to live by and work by, gleaned from my teachers—the managers I have interacted with over the years. These important "Thirteen Fundamentals that Matter" have served me well, and they can serve you well too. A number of them have been elaborated on elsewhere in these pages. They can increase (or nurture) your personal MQ*p*. And please take note: just because they are some of my basics pertaining to effective and rewarding management does not mean they are always easy to pursue or accomplish.

1. Practice compassion, humility, accessibility, and purposefulness.
2. Consider all stakeholders, not just owners—creating value for all.
3. Look to the horizon for possibilities and over your shoulder for lessons.
4. Honor the best of your organization's culture, history, norms, and values.
5. Be honest with everyone, including yourself, all the time.
6. Follow words with action, not more words.
7. Collaborate, communicate, and care whenever possible.
8. Be the most prepared in the meeting.
9. Practice and display stewardship, not entitlement.
10. Enhance the organization's comparative advantage as well as your own.
11. Find ways to make work satisfying and enjoyable for yourself and others.
12. Consider the unintended consequences of all performance metrics.
13. Share success broadly and frequently.

In concert with several colleagues and organizational clients, I have been involved in designing and developing scores of management development programs for corporate and governmental managers. To varying degrees, these thirteen fundamentals have been embedded in our final program designs and deliveries. That has been true whether it was a program for high-potential young managers or managers reporting to C-suite executives. And just like in a symphony when perhaps only a few brass instruments start and are subsequently joined by the entire brass section, followed later by the stringed instruments, during your career, some of these fundamentals will be front and center, then paired with others, while later, different ones may become the primary developmental focus. We can each compose a career by how we blend our learning and acquired expertise to create a beautiful arrangement of attributes, capabilities, and interests. Your challenge, my challenge, is to be known for the fundamentals we have blended, honed, and not deviated from for the benefit of our constituents.

REFLECT: *Conscientiously consider each of the thirteen management fundamentals. On a scale of zero to ten, with ten denoting a full-fledged adherence to it and zero conveying the complete absence of it in your management repertoire, rate yourself on each. For any item rated below five, why is there such a low rating? Do you not believe in that fundamental? If not, why not? Do you not have the requisite skills, patience, personality, and/or time to embrace it more fully? Which do you not have? Think about how that can be rectified. Take some time to reflectively craft your own list of management fundamentals that you want to keep top of mind and to be known for.*

_____

_____

_____

_____

IDENTIFY: *Pick one of the thirteen fundamentals you rated yourself the lowest on—or one of your own—and yet believe is important. Note two or three actions you could take to improve that part of your professional life. Also, pick one you rated yourself the highest on. In a humble way, would it be advantageous to you and/or your unit or organization to become known for excellence in that regard? Note two or three ideas for going about the task of* *becoming viewed by others as excellent in that regard.*

SHARE: *Invite a trusted colleague to lunch with the purpose of learning their opinion on the tasks you have tentatively laid out for yourself. Does the colleague agree with your self-assessment? Why or why not? If yes, does your action plan sound reasonable to them, or does it need adjustment? If no, what assessments of you, on the thirteen fundamentals (or on others you have identified for yourself), would they offer? What action plan(s) spring from those insights? This week, take some initial steps consistent with your final action plan.*

EVALUATE: *Were those initial action plan steps uncomfortable to take? Why? What would it take to make them a recurring part of your managerial approach? Can you commit to that? Why or why not? Don't forget your self-assessment on some of the other fundamentals. Do some of those also warrant your considered attention? What would it take to seek a high self-, peer-, or direct-report and boss-assessment on each? Codify your management fundamentals and commit to revisiting them from time to time.*

• • •

CHAPTER 6
Ideas for Action: Interpersonal-Focused
[vignettes #27–#36]

> **#27 Be alert! There are at least eleven different kinds of intelligence.**

Imagination is more important than knowledge.[81]

—ALBERT EINSTEIN,
winner of Nobel Prize for Physics

EDUCATORS AND ORGANIZATIONAL managers do not deny that people possess different kinds of aptitudes and skills and that those capabilities, across which they differ and excel, stretch beyond a traditional notion of school smarts. Think about that for a moment. It should, therefore, not come as any surprise that there is more than one type of intelligence that different people possess, improve, and use to craft careers of excellence, satisfaction, and high contribution. Indeed, there are at least eleven different intelligences: "factual, analytic, numerate, linguistic, spatial, athletic, intuitive, emotional, practical, interpersonal, and musical."[82]

The all-too-often reality is that organizations tend to shoehorn people with diverse intelligences into jobs that don't capitalize on those unique capabilities. To avoid such a circumstance creates the need for managers to understand the individual intelligence(s) needed for different jobs and then translate those most needed intelligences into appropriately tailored hiring, training, evaluation, and promotion practices. Over time, as employees accrue a life's worth of experiences, their interests and capabilities involving different intelligences also tend to evolve. Thus, managers need to avoid thinking of individuals in static, anchored ways.

Managers are well served to be in tune with the evolving preferences and competencies of their direct reports for two reasons. One is so that they can provide more satisfying opportunities for employees, which is likely to increase their level of satisfaction, contribution, and retention. A second reason is to provide assurance that the organization gets the best of what its people have to offer to enhance the organization's overall capabilities. Managers who excel do so because they find the right people with the right intelligence(s) doing what they are best at. Such managers insightfully and intentionally dovetail the rich variety of intelligences possessed by their people with the organizational challenges needing to be addressed and the opportunities to be pursued.

REFLECT: *Of the eleven intelligences listed, which ones best apply to you? Does your boss know this to be true about you? If not, why not? If yes, how has that shaped the responsibilities you have been given? Are you satisfied that your employer has fully utilized all the intelligences you possess? Are you in the process of honing additional intelligences, and if so, which ones, and if not, why not? Of the intelligences you believe you possess or are in the process of developing, which ones do not seem to have usefulness for your work? Can that be changed for mutual benefit? Do you want that to change? If not, why not, and if so, why?*

IDENTIFY: *What one personal area of intelligence would you like to play more of a role in your work life? Why, and what would that look like? Would that require a new job assignment, or could it be accomplished in your current position? Does it require you to take the initiative or your employer? Is there a way to pursue it with most of the impetus for change falling under your auspices? If so, what steps might that involve, and if not, what is in the way of that being true?*

SHARE: *At a conducive moment, perhaps during a casual coffee break or lunch, ask a colleague if they feel all their talents/ intelligences are being utilized, or are even known about, by your employer. Share with that person that you do not feel that it is true for you and that you would like to see some positive change in that regard. Share your idea for pursuing that positive change. How did they react? What did it spark in their own thinking for themselves? Did they see the mutual benefits possible? Were they encouraging, or did they discount your idea? Why? Commit to taking at least a few small steps along the path you laid out and may have tweaked based on their feedback.*

EVALUATE: *How did it go? Did the right people become more aware of all that you bring to the table? Were they surprised and pleased? Why or why not? Were there some things that you volunteered for that played to a broader array of your intelligences? If not, why not? What are you waiting for? If so, did you get at least a preliminary go-ahead? If not, why not? Can you sense an increase in your energy and engagement if you can get the green light to proceed? How hard are you prepared to push for those opportunities, all the while realizing that mutual benefit is the best kind to pursue?*

...ANOTHER CHAPTER 6 VIGNETTE...

> **#28 Be alert, again! Adults learn in particular ways.**

If you fail to prepare, you prepare to fail.[83]

—Pete Blaber,
former US Army Delta Force commander

LEARNING IS NOT, and cannot be, a "one-and-done" phenomenon. If it is, you are not merely treading water; you are losing ground to those around you who continue to learn. Yes, graduating from college or an apprenticeship is a significant milestone, but it merely signals some level of ability and aptitude to learn and, more importantly, perhaps, the beginning of a lifelong learning journey. As a manager, it is important to embrace that need for yourself and promote that same point to your direct reports, giving them the opportunity to do so. The work world and its management ranks need lifelong learners.

As a manager, besides knowing that there are different types of intelligences (see the previous vignette), it is also important to realize that different adults learn in different ways. Thus, some of your direct reports may learn in ways that differ from your predominant learning mode. In the work world especially, adult learners: [84]

- want to know why and what they need to learn,
- value self-directed and self-paced learning,
- use prior experiences to frame and aid their learning,

- discover more and more of what they don't know and need to know, thus becoming more open to learning,
- desire a line of sight that links what they are learning to their current needs/situation, and
- possess an intrinsic motivation due to a desire for career growth.

And your direct reports are at different places/stages pertinent to each of these six factors. Thus, the challenge for whomever is tasked with designing learning venues is finding that balance between individualized custom learning venues and a "one-size-fits-all" approach. Also, the goal is threefold—maximize learning, its retention, and its application.

It is true that there is some basic organizational information a company's personnel is required to learn—specific policies, regulations, and instructional how-tos. Self-paced online programs can be just fine for such learning needs. Professional development learning needs, however, are less suited to that approach. My view is that multiple-day residential learning programs, well-crafted and well-delivered, are most effective for a holistic and poignant approach to professional managerial development. In this dynamic setting, different means can be used at different times to tap into the different ways the adults in attendance are ready to learn.

As an example, consider the following features of a long-running, manager-level learning program that I have been privileged to lead. By its design, the learning opportunities provided for the adult managers in attendance to take advantage of include:

- identical reading assignments to be completed on an individual basis—mostly case studies depicting real-world management situations,
- selective use of simulations and computer-based analytical templates,
- repeated evening use of small group discussion teams,
- predominant use of facilitated class discussions with selective

use of lectures,
- learning topics linked back to learners' work environment,
- periodic use of small-group deliverables and/or presentations to reinforce commitments to apply the learning back at work,
- real-time, midclass breakout groups for immediate focus on applications and/or brainstorming,
- daily invitation to journal about that day's learning, links to work anticipated, and related to-dos when back in the office,
- selective use of outside expert speakers and/or Q&A panels, and
- program-ending, capstone declarations from each attendee regarding their key learning points and their key commitments for action upon returning to work.

These professional development program design and delivery elements are prompted by a concern for each of the six adult learning principles noted earlier. Moreover, they provide each learner the degrees of freedom conducive to individually prioritizing and applying lessons learned and insights gleaned as they best see fit. As a manager, knowing how your direct reports best learn can lead to the creation of more effective learning moments/venues resulting in more learning retained and applied.

REFLECT: *What are the features of a learning venue that are most appealing to you and most effective for you? Why? Can you answer the same question as it pertains to your direct reports? If not, why not? If so, in what ways are their learning preferences similar and dissimilar to yours? Might those dissimilarities be important? Why or why not? What are some of the customizable opportunities for learning that you are aware of for your direct reports? Should you seek out more information in that regard? If so, how? How much investment of time and money has been made in your personal professional development during the past* *two years? Is that enough? If not, why not? How much time and money has been invested in the professional development of your direct reports during the past two years? Is that enough? Why or why not? Would they each say that has been enough? Why or why not? Does your organization manifest a learning culture? If so, in what ways? If not, why not? If not, are you okay with that? Why or why not?*

_____
_____
_____
_____

IDENTIFY: *What specific learning agenda for yourself would you like to embark on, and why? What specific learning agenda for each of your key direct reports would you like to offer them, and why? Is there anything that precludes either of those thoughts coming to fruition in the next year? If so, what are the impediments, and what specific steps can you initiate to alleviate them?*

_____
_____
_____
_____

SHARE: *Make the case for the importance of learning as an organizational priority to a colleague. Do they agree? If yes, what might they add to that case? If not, why are they not in agreement? Share with them your desired personal professional learning agenda for the next year. Are they supportive? Why or* *why not? Share with them your learning priorities for your direct reports. Are they supportive? Why or why not? What would they add or subtract from those agendas, and why? Brainstorm with your colleague as to the potential case to be made to your bosses for establishing professional development as more of a priority (or being focused on different things) for the coming year than historically has been done or is currently planned.*

EVALUATE: *If you have raised the possibility of and need for more or different professional development for your direct reports with them, how did they receive that message? With their input, can you proceed to make that a reality for them? If not, why not? If so, devote some time and attention to making that a reality. How did it go? What sort of blended JIT (just-in-time) learning is most needed and appealing vis-à-vis JIC (just-in-case) learning? That blend may need to be different for different direct reports.*

...ANOTHER CHAPTER 6 VIGNETTE...

> **#29 *Look for opportunities to lead your peers.***

Leaders can be found at any rank and at any age.[85]

—General (ret.) Stanley McChrystal,
former commander of US and NATO forces in Afghanistan

MANAGERS ARE OFTEN called on to lead various organizational committees, task forces, or project teams, where those groups are comprised mostly of peers, not direct reports. Such an assignment presents the opportunity and challenge of leading via influence, respect, and collaboration rather than relying on the power and status associated with seniority, rank, or title.

In the arena of professional baseball, what an opportunity when a young pitcher makes his major league debut! What an opportunity when the prima ballerina understudy steps in for this week's performances! Both have the front-and-center opportunity to shine, leading their colleagues to an overall excellent result. Likewise, when a manager is tapped to lead a group of peers, it is an important, high-visibility opportunity to excel and to become known. The key question is . . . become known for what?

You may recall a series of very cleverly scripted and produced Farmers Insurance Company ads on television that ended with the tagline, "We know a thing or two because we've seen a thing or two." Indeed, we all learn from our own experiences as well as from those of others we have observed. In that spirit, and based on my experiences, a careful focus on the following six aspects of leading peers can help make such an opportunity more successful, more enjoyable, and perhaps more replicable for you. It may be useful to think of these six aspects with the acronym PRIMER[86]—key points for leading peers.

PROCESS

- Map out a sustainable, comfortable calendar of activities for the group of peers and share it with them at the outset.
- Establish key benchmarks toward the envisioned final deliverable.
- Identify and garner likely administrative resources needed.
- Acquire and share assurances from top organizational leaders that the group's deliverables will matter.
- Consider and discuss using subgroups for key tasks.

RESOLVE TO

- Learn about the talents and expertise of each group member.
- Clearly and promptly communicate what you see as each member's potential contribution(s) to the endeavor.
- Facilitate a conversation early on to surface and assess the merits of underlying assumptions that could potentially affect the group's stated task.
- Listen for the silence amongst the group throughout deliberations, resolving to find comfortable ways for all to participate and for "hard" things to be discussed.

INTEGRITY

- Be honest about what you don't know pertaining to the group's task and take appropriate steps to remedy that.
- Facilitate group deliberations that are transparent, inclusive, purposeful, confidential, and free of all sidebar agreements.
- Explicitly commit to the group's deliverables being a faithful

representation of the group's consensus, giving voice to any significant dissenting views.

MINDSET
- Be humble and listen well.
- Share any spotlight moments and take any blame.
- Look for valid occasions to celebrate group (or individual) effort or results.

EXCITEMENT/ENERGY
- Do not accept the leader role if you are not excited by the purpose of the endeavor.
- Fuel group energy by articulating the potential organizational benefits resulting from the group's stated mission.
- Share stories of how prior groups have succeeded, operated, and delivered beneficial outcomes for the organization.

RESPECT
- Exhibit respect for staff, group members, organizational leaders, and the mission for which the group has been tasked.
- Strive to accommodate the prior commitments of group members.
- Acknowledge, discuss, and evaluate pertinent precedence pertaining to the group's task.
- Value the group's investment of effort, time, and energy by NOT steering outcomes to a predetermined outcome.

Let's be honest—leading and managing a group of peers, even if for a short-lived project, can be a bit intimidating. To do so successfully is both a personally gratifying experience and a de facto audition for subsequently larger organizational responsibilities. Being accepted as a leader of peers is one of the most rewarding aspects of a high-performing team you are likely to experience. Indeed, doing so successfully contributes to a positive sense of having made a notable contribution, both personally and collectively.

> **REFLECT:** *Off and on, over the next couple of days, think of a time when you led a group of peers. That experience might have been at work, for a community organization, or even as captain of a high school sports team. What do you recollect most about that experience? What lessons can you glean from that in hindsight? What was the most challenging part of that experience, and why? What could you have done better in that role? Why and how? Similarly, recall an example of one of your peers being cast in that role that you were privy to observing. What did they do well and not so well in leading you? Think in terms of the PRIMER dimensions to stimulate your reflections and focus.*
>
> _____
> _____
> _____
> _____
>
> **IDENTIFY:** *There will likely be more opportunities to lead peers. Based on your takeaways from your reflections above, try crafting a one-page personal Leading Peers Memo. Start with a clear, aspirational statement of what you want that leadership opportunity to be like for you and for those that you will lead. Next, explicitly state the values you want to espouse and model throughout that assignment. Then, articulate, in general terms, how you are inclined to want to tackle the tasks and goals to be pursued. Finish the memo with a clear statement as to what you want the completed experience to have succeeded in accomplishing for the team and the organization. If, perchance, you have a*

leading-peers opportunity that is just commencing, this personal Leading Peers Memo can be tailored and detailed to that task.

_____

_____

_____

_____

SHARE: *Your personal Leading Peers Memo could serve as a stimulus and model for others. Conscientious forethought, prior to a pending leading-peers assignment and opportunity, is time and effort well spent. Talk to a couple of colleagues about your desire to be very intentional and thoughtful in approaching such opportunities. Do they agree with you that it is an important opportunity? Would they, too, like to be more intentional and thoughtful in that regard? If not, why not? If yes, share with them your personal Leading Peers Memo. Ask for feedback on that memo, noting that it is a personalized version and is intended to serve as your own reminder of commitments for leading peers.*

_____

_____

_____

_____

EVALUATE: *Refine your Leading Peers Memo based on the inputs from colleagues. Does it now highlight all that you want it to, and does it convey both a sense of preparedness and anticipation? It should. After your next opportunity to lead a group of peers, how did the exercise of crafting that memo help you do a better job in leading them? Make it a dynamic* *document—update/revise it after each leading-peers opportunity has begun or has been completed. Be thoughtfully intentional and anticipatory in how you approach an opportunity to lead peers.*

_____
_____
_____
_____
_____

... ANOTHER CHAPTER 6 VIGNETTE ...

> **#30 Teams usually perform best under pressure or with a high calling.**

... pairing old solutions with new problems is the worst way to run a team.[87]

—Robert O'Neill,
US Navy Seal credited with killing Osama Bin Laden

OVER THE YEARS, I have probably asked 300 or more managers to recall a time when they were part of a highperforming team. Frequently, their initial, strongest memories do not pertain to processes or specifics but rather to the collaborations enjoyed, the sense of being on mission they felt, and the significance of the purpose/objective the team achieved.[88]

Whether the team was a championship sports team, a fundraising committee for a favorite not-for-profit, a new product development group, or a team putting together a proposal for a prospective client, the managers articulated a clear, palpable, heightened sense of commitment that drew the members of the team together in an exciting, memorable way. Perhaps the stakes were high (e.g., $10 million proposal or a state championship), or time was short for a key task (e.g., a rampaging forest fire or a looming deadline), or the goal strongly desired (e.g., a new building for the church or a technological problem you are sure *can* be solved) that the group of individuals became so galvanized, so focused, and so seamlessly compatible that they were transformed from an assembled group into an extraordinary team. Indeed, senses come alive, creative juices flow, energy seems limitless, clarity of purpose shines brightly, and individuals interact in mutually sustaining ways. Whether you read accounts of the New York City response team operating in the wake of the 9/11 attacks, watch the NASA team in *Apollo 13*, or simply ask yourself about the hallmark of a personal high-performance team experience, chances are you will note a common denominator amongst those stories: a clear sense of at-stakeness, pressure to come through, and a motivating purpose. Without that, teams can lose focus and commitment. With some purpose-related pressure, amazing things can be accomplished, and feelings of accomplishment, togetherness, and mission proudly take their place on one's mantel of fond memories and desired replication. Team members integrate their best efforts with those of their colleagues, they strongly share a clear sense of purpose in undertaking a difficult task, and each team member succeeds when the team succeeds.

Healthy pressure for a team arises from a meaningful mission that requires excellent outcomes. Unhealthy pressure for a team is rooted in unrealistic deadlines, inadequate resources, and/or poor leadership. No pressures for a team stem from routinized work, predetermined outcomes, and trivial purposes. Volunteer for the first scenario—meaningful mission—not the latter two. If you are leading a team, create the former context, not the latter two. Build a résumé and a memory bank of high-performance team experiences that fuel feelings in hindsight of a job and effort well done, of having risen to take on a tough task that was energizing to tackle and an experience you wouldn't trade for just about anything else. To want this is not a prideful thing—it is a pleasing, "I mattered, we mattered, we did it!" sort of feeling. Seek it out.

REFLECT: *Think back over your personal and professional life to identify a time when you were part of a high-performing* *team. (If you can't think of such an experience, recollect one that you believe came the closest or one that had the potential to become one but never did.) Perhaps it was a special project team at work, a certain high school band performance, a college theater production, or a recent charity fundraiser. For the specific remembrance that comes to mind, what aspects do you recall most powerfully and fondly? If it was an experience that fell short, why did it fall short? What was missing? Do you anticipate more high-performance team experiences in the future, and if so, why, and if not, why not? If not, would you like to?*

_____
_____
_____
_____

IDENTIFY: *What needs to happen, or be in place, so that at least once during the next twelve months, your odds of being part of a high-performing team are greatly increased? Should you be more proactive in volunteering for certain team assignments? Do you need to more vigilantly scan the organizational landscape for such opportunities? Is there someone you need to inform of your interest in this regard, and if so, who? What do you need to do to be available, ready, and known as interested in the next opportunity for a potential high-performing team experience?*

_____
_____
_____
_____

SHARE: *With all the enthusiasm of your recollected high-performing team memory fresh in your mind, share with a friend or colleague what that remembrance is and your desire for more of that sort of experience. How did they react? Do they have a basis for sharing a similar sentiment? If not, you might be in a prime position to sell them on the prospects and the value of such an experience, and if so, give that a shot. Share with them how you plan to make yourself available, ready, and known for an interest in such an endeavor. Does it seem reasonable and feasible to them? If not, why not? Digest their feedback and consider if you need to modify your proactive approach accordingly.*

_____

_____

_____

_____

EVALUATE: *After having undertaken some of the steps in your plan to become available, ready, and known for wanting a high-performing team experience (at work or elsewhere), what kind of progress have you made? Are you ready and available? If not, why not? How were your outreach overtures received by others? Do you feel encouraged or discouraged, and why? Have potentially high-performance teams been created without you being invited? If so, consider asking the sponsor of those teams why you were not selected. Find out what you need to do to further prepare yourself for such an opportunity. Based on your fond recollections of your prior experiences in this regard, you know it is worth pursuing.*

_____

_____

... ANOTHER CHAPTER 6 VIGNETTE ...

> **#31 What can someone bring? The TEA$^{(squared)}$, of course.**

> *... the making of tea became a visual metaphor for carrying on [in the midst of WWII] ... as long as there was tea, there was England. Tea underpinned morale.*[89]
>
> —Erik Larson,
> author of numerous *New York Times* bestsellers.

THINK ABOUT YOURSELF, your direct reports, and your organization's other personnel. From an overarching vantage point, they all come to work with their hands, their heads, and their hearts. And an organization should want all three to be robustly (if not fully) engaged each day. It is difficult to disconnect or isolate these three facets of a person. Astute managers want employees' doing (hands), thinking (head), and motivated by a sense of mission (heart).

With a group of about forty-five managers in a hotel conference room one Friday morning, I challenged them to focus on these three aspects of the people who worked for them. Together, we embarked on a discussion to ascertain the foundational underpinnings of what a manager can expect to get from their employees' hands, heads, and hearts. Over a couple hours, the brainstorming ended, the discussion wound down, and our final task was to synthesize and codify all that had been posed. The consensus was that the essence of what everyone brings to work boiled down to our *t*ime, *t*alent, *e*nergy, *e*ffort, *a*ttitude, and *a*spirations—TEA$^{(squared)}$.

Time

Consider these sobering statistics[90]:

> "89% of workers admit to wasting time every day at work. 31% of workers waste at least one hour at work every day. U.S. employees spend an average of 2.9 hours per 8-hour workday doing non-work activities. The average employee spends 21.5 hours in meetings every week and attends 62 meetings every month. 64% of employees admit to visiting non-work-related websites at work every day."

Moreover, think about another sobering phenomenon pertaining to the workforce. "Quiet quitting"[91] is when someone is still employed and present but doing only the bare minimum level of work. The "fix" for any of these conditions is not more monitoring or rules. The "fix" is to create opportunities for more engagement, enjoyment, and success at work.

Talent

"People who choose not to apply their talents [at work] are often bored, angry, lazy, distracted, or lacking the spark to become engaged in their work."[92] And, I will add, they might be assigned to do work that does not adequately tap nor stretch their talents. Informal, preplanned, and explicitly focused conversations can pose questions along these lines to identify possible root causes for the underutilization of someone's talents whom you know, as their manager, have more to offer.

Energy

Energy fuels effort. Physical energy undergirds stamina throughout the day and an aura of "let's go, we can do this, lean in." Mental energy contributes to alertness, concentration, the curiosity to learn, and the consideration of new possibilities. Emotional energy establishes and nurtures the strength and duration of connection between people and between a person and the role they play in furthering the mission of their employer. All three types of energy are important, contagious, beneficial, and, frankly, justifiably expected by managers.

Effort

"Effort is how hard we try."[93] It is evidenced by the level of time, talent, and energy brought to bear at what an employee is tasked with doing. Minimal effort results in minimal engagement. Extensive effort results in doing what is expected and going beyond. Indeed, extensive effort is manifested by frequent organizational prospecting—exploring and searching for ways to contribute beyond basic expectations and assignments.

Attitude

Attitude is the mindset with which one views their work, colleagues, and organization. A positive attitude is eager, cheerful, optimistic, and sees the best in colleagues, work, and organizational mission. A negative attitude is insidious for the one harboring such an attitude and toxic for those interacting with that person. It devalues colleagues, work, and organizational mission. It diminishes the person's desire and ability to devote needed and expected levels of time, talent, and effort to their tasks. There is a third mode of attitude that is potentially detrimental—a checked-out attitude. This person, akin to a "quiet quitter," does their job at an okay level, may tend to exhibit a loner preference for collegiality, refrains from learning, and can ultimately manifest an entitled attitude that pits them against colleagues and/or the organization.

Aspirations

I don't think most people in their twenties or even their thirties can comprehend what it means to have a career of forty or more years. That is a long time to simply go through the motions of doing one's tasks and collecting a paycheck. If much of our life is spent working and we want to enjoy and feel fulfilled to some degree by the time devoted to work, a person's aspirations should not be checked at their employer's front door. Work should be an outlet for some significant personal and professional aspirations. Aspirations can be big or small, simple or complex, constant or evolving, missional or relational. A valid aspiration might simply be that I want to help one of my colleagues do a certain task better this week. Or it might be that I want to make progress on developing improved safety protocols for our delivery drivers. Or it might be that I want to contribute to improving the morale of my accounting department. Aspirations are inspirational and are the tangible manifestations of one's values. Managers are well served in becoming informed about the aspirations of their direct reports and facilitating opportunities for those to be pursued.

Diagnosing the TEA$^{\text{(squared)}}$ levels of yourself, a cohort, a team, or an entire workforce is a task to consider. My colleague Jim Clawson and I have developed and used an instrument to help with such an assessment. That detailed instrument, titled *Managing the Career Blues*, is available from the University of Virginia's Darden Graduate School of Business case materials store, https://store.darden.virginia.edu/WidgetsSearch/SearchText?Q=pacs-0097 (accessed 5-29-24). Assessing an employee's levels on these six TEA$^{\text{(squared)}}$ factors is helpful in ascertaining where that employee is likely to fall on a continuum from high career engagement through a midrange level indicative of modest to perhaps even severe career blues, all the way down to career disengagement. Knowing the TEA$^{\text{(squared)}}$ health of your direct reports just might unlock some value-added possibilities for them, for you, and for the organization.

REFLECT: *[Note: I recommend obtaining and using the instrument noted above in the following discussion. In its absence,* *the suggested approach below constitutes a viable start for assessing and using insights from a TEA$^{(squared)}$ diagnosis.]*

On a scale of 1 to 10, with 10 being excellent and 1 being very poor, rate each of the TEA$^{(squared)}$ factors for yourself. As a general heuristic and starting point, any rating less than 8 warrants evaluation. For any rating you have below 8, why is that rating not 8 or higher? Do you sincerely want it to be 8 or higher, and can it become 8 or higher? If yes, what needs to happen? If not, why not? Are there circumstances in your personal life that account for those lower-than-desired ratings?

Perform a similar rating for each of your direct reports, simply from your own vantage point. For any ratings less than 8, give some serious thought to what might need to change for that person for you to ultimately boost that rating and how you might be able to facilitate that change. If numerous direct reports exhibit similarly low ratings for identical factors, what might systemically account for that?

_____

_____

_____

_____

_____

IDENTIFY: *For yourself, what one or two to-dos surface to raise any self-ratings to 8 or above? If all your self-ratings were initially 8 or above, what to-dos arise to boost any or all of them to the next higher level?*

For your direct reports, were there any indications of possible systemic issues warranting your conscientious managerial attention? If so, what are the initial steps to be taken in that regard? If not, zero in on one or two of your direct reports with multiple ratings less than 8. What action(s) on your part come to mind as viable and important to help them be/do better at work?

___

SHARE: *Consider giving each of your direct reports the $TEA^{(squared)}$ factor descriptions and ask them to rate themselves on each of those six factors in the context of their work. Review their self-ratings and compare them with the ratings you assigned them for the same factor. Any of their self-ratings below 8 warrants a developmental discussion, as does any difference of 2 or more between your ratings and theirs. The purpose of any such discussion is to enhance your understanding of them and their situation along with, where appropriate, offering to be of assistance. In this latter regard, it is important to offer only what you truly can deliver—promises that you cannot fulfill help no one.*

___

EVALUATE: *How did the discussions with some of your direct reports go? Were they helpful to you and to them? Why or why not? Did they buy into the $TEA^{(squared)}$ factors as worthy of focus and development? Why or why not? As a result of those discussions, what are your expectations? What foci and expectations do you have for your development along those six factors? Have you begun that developmental process? If not, why not?*

WHAT IF YOU TRIED THIS AT WORK?

... ANOTHER CHAPTER 6 VIGNETTE ...

> **#32 *Empowerment requires enablement and encouragement.***

Keep away from people who try to belittle your ambitions. Small people always do that, but the really great make you feel that you, too, can become great.[94]

—Mark Twain,
author and American humorist

ONE OF THE most overused words in organizational circles must be "empowerment" and its various versions. At some level, managers know that empowerment is when bosses expect direct reports to take the initiative. Resident, in that notion, is the tacit understanding of not having to ask for permission. All too often, that also means accountability, consequences, and even blame if things do not quite turn out right (where "right" might be defined after the fact). It is incumbent on organizations to prepare their people for empowered decision-making. Just as we do not learn to swim by being thrown in the deep end of the pool (contrary to popular folklore), organizational members must possess the accumulated capabilities that maximize the likelihood of success on the initiatives pursued under the mantle of empowerment.

How does someone acquire the knowledge and skills to be best prepared for taking empowered initiative? The answer to this question is through one or more of the following means: (a) the accumulation of pertinent key experiences, (b) a rich array of JIT (just-in-time) and JIC (just-in-case) management development instruction, and (c) through targeted coaching and ongoing constructive performance review feedback.

Many seasoned managers agree that accumulated key experiences position rising managers best for seizing the initiative and thus operating in an empowered manner. Conscientious consideration of the types of key experiences to be accumulated is a significant aspect of becoming empowered. In working with the chief human resources officer of a *Fortune* 500 company, a colleague and I identified eleven key experiences that, if accomplished well, increase the odds for a manager to be successful in exercising their empowerment and to ultimately become executive-level candidates.[95] The first seven pertain to *what* key experiences are important to have.

1. Serve customers and/or clients well.
2. Grow an important part of the organization.
3. Develop a global mindset.
4. Know the various parts of your organization and how they interact.
5. Leverage technology.
6. Contribute to building an organization's talent pool.
7. Lead a part of an organization or a major organizational project.

The next four key experiences signal *how* to best accomplish the first seven.

8. Create a climate for success in the arenas in which you have had responsibility.
9. Demonstrate an inspirational shared vision.
10. Lead a significant organizational change.
11. Preach and practice collaboration for mutual benefit.

The eleven foci above help establish a manager's capability to effectively exercise their empowerment. They contribute to achieving *enablement*. *Encouragement* is the other important dimension undergirding meaningful empowerment. Encouragement can take many forms, both planned and spontaneous. Words of encouragement take on true meaning when successful initiative-taking is affirmed, celebrated, and made known to others in the organization. Organizations that model punishment-free approaches for good decision-making that results in unfortunate outcomes will also foster reasonable risk-taking, which is an important mindset for those with new, and perhaps even novel, ideas to better the organization. Failures should lead to personal learning as well as organizational learning. In fact, Jim Mattis, a former US Secretary of Defense and a retired Marine Corps general, has noted that "A commander . . . must be tolerant of mistakes. If the risk takers are punished, then you will retain in your ranks only the risk averse."[96]

Organizational oral histories, exemplifying empowered employees striving to make the organization better, can also be effectively used to further encourage an empowerment mindset. Importantly, oral histories can testify to a culture that believes empowerment is a foundational element of developing and preserving an entrepreneurial spirit amongst employees. Furthermore, an organizational norm for working in small collaborative groups can be used to underscore the importance of empowered initiative-taking. Empowered collaboration can not only fuel the promulgation of ideas, but it can also provide checks and balances to curb unwarranted risk-taking.

REFLECT: *Do you feel empowered in your job? Why or why not? Are you okay with the level of empowerment at work that you believe you have? Why or why not? Do you feel that you are prepared to astutely exercise whatever level of empowerment the organization has given you? Why or why not? In your job, have you exercised the freedom you have been empowered with, and if not, why not? If yes, what transpired, and what is your takeaway* *from that experience? Would you like to have more empowerment? Why or why not? Would you like to offer more empowerment to your direct reports? Why or why not? Are you unsure if your boss is supportive of you taking informed risks? Why or why not? What is your personal appetite for risk-taking?*

_____
_____
_____
_____
_____

IDENTIFY: *What key experiences are lacking in your portfolio that you believe would make you a more effective and prepared user of the empowerment you have been given or the empowerment you desire? Why those? Prioritize them and flesh out what you see as pertinent to each for your own personal development. What new (or additional) personal and/or organizational factors would increase your courage in being a bit more of a conscientious risk taker at work, and why those factors? What sort of clarity do you want from your boss about your authority to act in an empowered, initiative-seizing, modest risk-taking manner? Apply each of these questions to your direct reports. What are the action items that surface for you as their manager?*

_____
_____
_____
_____
_____

SHARE: *In your next regularly scheduled performance review* or *"stay interview"* with your boss, raise the issues and thoughts you identified above. Seek a conversation with them on those issues to garner encouragement, obtain clarity on any pertinent parameters, and hear the stories of their exercising empowerment and venturing into well-informed risk-taking. As a result of your conversation: (a) recalibrate your risk-taking inclination as needed/desired, (b) request an opportunity for obtaining the key experiences you prioritized as #1 and #2, and (c) exercise some organizational scanning for identifying examples of, and lessons emanating from, the exercise of empowerment and astute risk-taking—i.e., start building an organizational oral history of empowerment stories. Touch base with one or two direct reports. Pose for them your thoughts about potentially beneficial and pertinent key experiences you'd like them to have. Do they agree? Why or why not?

_____

_____

_____

_____

_____

EVALUATE: *At an appropriate future point in time, ask yourself if you are ready to manage in a more empowered way. Why are you ready/willing to do so, or why are you not? In the meantime, have you addressed the empowerment of your direct reports with an eye toward making them more enabled-capable and more aware of your willingness to assist and encourage them? If not, why not? If yes, how has it progressed? Be prepared to learn from all the empowerment-fueled, astute risk-taking initiatives that you and your direct reports have taken. Share those lessons in ways that will benefit a wider cohort of colleagues and direct reports.*

WHAT IF YOU TRIED THIS AT WORK?

...ANOTHER CHAPTER 6 VIGNETTE...

> *#33 Whenever possible, be more relational and less transactional.*

You wonder why there's no word for the opposite of lonely.[97]

—Pam Houston,
American award-winning author

SEVERAL COLLEAGUES AND I were invited to study three different world-class professional services firms to identify the factors giving rise to their renowned, successful use of collaborative teams to address client issues. As we conducted our numerous interviews, it was obvious from the outset that each of these premiere firms challenged the stereotype of a collection of selfcentered individual performers. These firms had moved beyond the notion of teams as merely a means for task-oriented, event-centered, transactional collaboration to a broader, deeper, more enduring notion of teaming with a commitment to what we termed relational collaboration. The distinction between these two types of collaboration can be summarized as: [98]

	Collaboration Type	
	Transactional	Relational
Timing	episodic	continuous
Focus	project/task	person

	Collaboration Type	
	Transactional	**Relational**
Foundation	roles	shared values
Key Activity	coordination	partnering
Dependency	roles/task fit	person/organization fit

In our conversations with members of these organizations, we ascertained that there were three person-centered and three organization-based factors that enabled them to evolve to relational collaboration as a distinguishing feature of their client service and internal teaming. Members of these firms all exhibited (1) a calling for their career choice, (2) a caring attitude for clients, colleagues, and their work and (3) a creative mindset and drive. From the organization's perspective, each firm exhibited (1) a coherent mission and strategy clearly communicated to all, (2) a set of congruent information systems used as a guide in pursuing their mission and strategy, and (3) a willingness to make sizable investments in learning for their people and for bringing their people together on a regular, face-to-face basis. The essence of their relational collaboration was that an entire organization behaved like a high-performance team; that is, the dynamics of a committed small group were replicated at the organizational scale.[99]

How were they able to develop and preserve their strong and distinctive internal, relational, collaborative culture? The partners of a large, global, prestigious Wall Street investment banking firm often cited the concerted efforts their global network of partners made to physically get together. They told us they consciously sought to rotate the location of management meetings, they committed to regular attendance at numerous professional development venues, and they often took advantage of temporary assignment invitations from other offices. In an era of electronic communications and virtual meetings, it is critical to personally connect. The managers in this firm were willing to invest the time and money to make it a priority. Indeed, Charles Handy has noted that "Trust needs touch" and "Paradoxically, the more virtual an organization becomes, the more its people need to meet in person."[100]

Likewise, in a conversation with a senior trial attorney at the large and well-respected law firm we studied, I was impressed when he unabashedly referred to his fellow partners as "foxhole lawyers." He went on to explain that by that phrase, he meant that he felt an affinity for his colleagues that went beyond merely that of being fellow workers. There was real affection, respect, and trust. Their collaborations were foundationally built on a set of longstanding, shared relationships. Each colleague brought something unique to the pooled relationship and had invested the time to get to know what their colleagues specialized in and how it dovetailed with their and others' skills. Each was proud of the firm, proud of their part in it, and proud of their colleagues. Members of the firm shared an incredible sense of collective potential. They had progressed beyond a mere collection of individuals, each doing their own thing. They had elevated collaboration beyond the intra-team level to the intra-firm level. They were there for each other, for the firm. They frequently and selflessly aided and inspired one another, not fretting about who had originated or landed a client. Helping one another helped the firm, which improved the business for everyone.

REFLECT: *Do you have some "foxhole friends" at work? Are you mostly a get-it-done-and-move-on-to-the-next-task type person, or do you frequently make the effort to get to know the people you are working with a bit better? Why do you think your tendency is as you just noted? Do you ask relationally-oriented questions not directly applicable to the task at hand? Why or why not? How do you tend to respond to such questions asked of you, and why? How well would you say you know your direct* *reports? Your managerial colleagues? Your boss(es)? Your external constituents (e.g., key customers/clients/donors, vendors, sales/ philanthropy reps, community leaders, bankers)? Has that level of familiarity produced friendships? In your mind, do you have enough friends, or do you want to keep your professional and personal lives separate? Why? Can you enumerate several ways that a closer relationship with others in the above-named groups would be beneficial to you and your organization? If you can, are those facets worth pursuing and nurturing? If not, why not? Would you like to be better known by any of the above-named constituents? Why or why not?*

_____

_____

_____

_____

IDENTIFY: *The reflection questions above seek to shed light on your approach to the people you encounter in your work. If we are generally not prone to reflection or are extremely busy, we do not take stock of how we interact with others at work, and before we know it, our personal default way of interactions takes root, and we find ourselves swept along in that mode. If you are satisfied with your level of relational interactions with various constituencies based on your reflections above, that is your choice—you are now aware. If you are not satisfied, what two or three things can you commit to doing differently, starting tomorrow, to become more relational? For me, it has been useful to think of the people I encounter during my work as valued partners with a shared interest and interesting life stories, not just a job doer, a means to an end. "Means to an end" will get the task done, but I believe it will be less enjoyable, less meaningful, and* *less impactful than it might otherwise have been.*

_____

_____

_____

_____

SHARE: *If you have made a personal commitment to become more relational in your managerial endeavors, share that commitment and what you plan to do in that regard with a colleague. Are they surprised? Why or why not? Are they encouraging? Why or why not? Are there a couple of managers in your organization that you would both agree are very relational in their approach to work? If so, what do you both see as some of the hallmarks of how they do what they do, and are those aspects replicable? Why or why not? Spend a full week conscientiously practicing being more relational in your interactions and less transactional. Yes, work needs to be done and done well, but that does not preclude bringing a relational dimension to bear in that work.*

_____

_____

_____

_____

EVALUATE: *How did it go? Did you enjoy those pauses, those moments to get to know someone a bit better? Did it enrich the exchange? Did it enrich your day? If so, in what way(s)? If not, why not? Were you wholehearted and authentic in your relational moments and conversations? Why or why not? Did you ask more questions of them than talking about* *yourself? Were you a bit trepidatious about crossing some unseen or known boundary? If so, why? Might the answer to this final question warrant some organization-wide conversations about norms, values, boundaries, and how best to be relational and respectful at work? If so, surface that need at a management meeting for discussion.*

_____
_____
_____
_____
_____

. . . ANOTHER CHAPTER 6 VIGNETTE . . .

> #34 *Find and show your softer side.*

> *. . . gratitude is an appropriate response to almost everything.*[101]
>
> —Pam Houston,
> American award-winning author

"MARK, YOUR NAME is not going to be put forth by the nominating committee to the full board for the board president position. Your tough-minded ways are viewed as being just too hard-hearted. Sorry." Such was the message conveyed to me in a phone call I got one evening. *Wow . . . hard-hearted?* This not-for-profit organization had been in some tough financial circumstances, and I had no idea that my willingness to make some pointed recommendations had been viewed as hard-hearted. In hindsight, I fear that in the months leading up to that moment, I had not exhibited enough of my more caring, considerate, humble side to offset the perceived hard-heartedness of the suggestions I had made.

Let's fruitfully digress for just a moment. You have been engaged in research and experimentation your entire life. As a baby, you cried to get attention. It worked. In elementary school, you probably conducted sanctioned and unsanctioned experiments. My first sanctioned research was to light a match, drop it into the bottom of a milk bottle, and immediately place a hard-boiled egg over the opening.

Wait a few seconds, and voilà, the match used up all the oxygen in the bottle, creating a vacuum that sucked the egg into the bottle. Very cool to a seven-year-old. My unsanctioned research was finding out if, when Johnny shot his new BB gun at close range into the palm of my hand, it would hurt. It did. In high school, you probably tried flirting in different ways until you snagged the boyfriend/girlfriend you thought you wanted. In college, you may have tested the limits of skipping classes and still getting a decent grade in a course. As an adult, you have encountered and met hundreds, if not thousands, of other people. In doing so, you have noted your reactions to them—you liked some, others not; were intrigued by some, others not; impressed by some, others not; and some you wanted to get to know better, others not. You have read books and watched movies, all with various characters moving through the story. Some of those characters you related to, others not; some you cheered for, others not; some you wished were real and lived next door, others not. Unconsciously, and perhaps even consciously, your reactions have been in response to what you are most drawn to in others and what you want to be associated with in life. Indeed, our closest friends are those who possess the traits we most value in a friend.

    I have thought a lot about what I find most appealing in the people I meet, whether at work or elsewhere. There are four traits that keep coming to the fore of my reflections: competency, authenticity, curiosity about and care for others, and vulnerability. For me, these traits in others trump the things they may have accomplished/accumulated, the personal pedigree they possess, the title they use, and the position they hold. I certainly respect the latter two, and yet, on a stand-alone basis, those two do not evoke any more warmth, affection, or interest from me than people without position or title. After many years, I have concluded that those traits I am most drawn to are perhaps some of the same traits that others would value and be drawn to in me. Thus, I have tried my best to become that sort of person. There is, of course, room for the differences that add Technicolor, tone, and texture to my life, and yet, those four core attributes are priorities for me. I have come to that realization somewhat late in life—and unfortunately, well after the nonprofit's nominating committee labeled me hard-hearted.

Yes, a manager sometimes needs to make tough decisions with courage and fortitude. When those decisions affect people, however, they can still be made with managerial authenticity and care and without an arrogant show of detached resolve or callous concern. Many managers tap into personal beliefs related to life's higher duty, higher calling, an ethic of behavior that dampens self-interest. For example, those subscribing to the philosophical school of *universalism* subscribe to the key personal traits of respectfulness for others, fairness, cooperativeness, compassion, spiritual respect, and humility.[102] For those embracing Christianity, the key personal traits to be manifested are love, joy, peace, patience, kindness, goodness, faithfulness, gentleness, and self-control.[103] In the Jewish tradition, the seven "special qualities that drive [the human soul] and enrich it [are] . . . transcendence, vitality, joy, awareness, action, struggle, and tranquility."[104] Similarly, the Jewish philosophy of "Musar" highlights thirteen "soul traits" for virtuous living: humility, patience, enthusiasm, trust, loving-kindness, truth, honor, gratitude, order, silence, equanimity, fear, and awe.[105] These traits are not intended to pose multiple choice options, applicable in some settings and not others or pertinent for some people you interact with and not for others. Whatever the catalyst for setting aside self-interest, hubris, and callousness, let it be your persona at work, to the fullest extent possible, not just outside of work. Take your deepest true self with you wherever you go.

The Salvation Army, KIND, Chick-fil-A, Inc., and American Color, Inc. are but four among many organizations that clearly espouse values they want to guide their purpose and their daily activities. Listen to your inner voice and sense the resonance, the pleasure, the uplifting nature of those appeals to a higher calling registering inside you. Don't discount or dismiss that inner voice. Don't leave it at home when you go to work. Don't ignore the direction it signals for you. Vow to never be thought of as hard-hearted!

REFLECT: *What characteristics in others are you most drawn to, and why? As you call those traits to mind, are you thinking of colleagues or people outside the workplace? Wouldn't it be great if many of them were work colleagues? Are you conscious of manifesting those same desirable attributes to those around you? Why or why not? Do you want to? Why or why not? Do you feel that since you are a manager, you cannot and should not exhibit "soft" traits such as doubt, vulnerability, compassion, forgiveness, and patience in combination with your "hard" skills such as analytics, systems thinking, process design, and financial literacy? Why or why not? Can you be a great manager and still exhibit vulnerability? Can you be a performance-oriented manager and still practice patience and forgiveness? Can you make tough personnel decisions and still be compassionate? Yes, you can! Do you want to?*

_____
_____
_____
_____

IDENTIFY: *On a scale of 1 to 10, with 1 being "not at all," rate how well you believe your direct reports know your softer, nontechnical, nonanalytical, non-process-focused side. Is that the level of "knowingness" you want? Why or why not? What one or two "softer" aspects of your personality would you like them to see and know better? Why, and how can you best bring* *that awareness about? Sequence through these same questions in relation to your colleagues and then again in relation to your boss.*

SHARE: *In a fast-paced, performance-mandated, deliverables-oriented environment, the softer side of our being is often checked at the door and set aside. Meet with a friend and discuss your desire to bring more fully your spiritual-based and/or humanity-centered qualities to bear in the workplace and the means for doing that. Listen carefully to their reactions and inputs. End that meeting with a purposeful path for becoming more fully known by your direct reports, colleagues, and boss. In my experience, such a journey will be well received by others or, at worst, with ambivalence. Thus, there is nothing to lose on that front. But you are likely to find yourself more fully engaged at work and with work, more attuned to the rhythms and culture of that environment and fulfilled with a sense of "Here is who I am." Being known in that fuller light is a positive place to be.*

EVALUATE: *Has there been more of your whole/true self present and observable at work than before because of the* *path you committed to above? Why or why not? What have you encountered from others in reaction to transparently bringing more of yourself to the workplace? Has that been encouraging or discouraging, and why? Are you tempted in any way to shrink back from bringing more of your whole self to bear, including your softer side, to work? Why or why not? Does one constituency appear to value your softer side more than another? If so, why? In your heart of hearts and with your workplace in mind, who do you want to be, and for now, which constituent group do you want to honor most with your full self? Why?*

_____
_____
_____
_____
_____

... ANOTHER CHAPTER 6 VIGNETTE ...

> **#35 *Consider making care a core strength.***

*It is love that makes us willing to sacrifice,
love that gives us courage.*[106]

—John McCain,
former US senator (AZ) and Vietnam War POW

AT A WORKPLACE retirement celebration for a colleague, along with several others, I was asked to offer a few words of fond farewell. I readily accepted the invitation and made some sincere remarks on that occasion. What I most remember about that privilege, however, came at the very end of my time with the microphone. My final words were "I love you." They just came out. They were not planned or scripted. At that moment of closing, and as my gaze met his, those three words came out. Wow, that was unexpected. I had never heard those three words uttered in the hallways of that organization ... ever! And, as the subsequent casual reception got underway, a different senior manager colleague came up to me and said something to the effect of "I hope someone says that to me during their retirement speech for me."

After the retirement gathering, as I thought more about the spontaneity of the "I love you" moment and the hope expressed by my other colleague, I realized that love and caring have a valuable place in organizations. It is something we all respond favorably to. Sincere caring from those in management positions can bolster the dedication and resilience of others, fuel energized engagement, foster a sense of purpose and mission within teams, and provide the glue that creates dedicated bonds between colleagues.

Care in the workplace for one's direct reports and colleagues can be exhibited by, among other things:

- helping others, especially direct reports, become known within and across established networks,
- inquiring about their nonwork-related interests and passions,
- seizing opportunities to celebrate their accomplishments (work-related or not),
- providing them with assistance (with no strings attached) when needed and not even asked for,
- avoiding assumptions that pose the worst about them when performance is down, and seek them out to find out why as soon as possible,
- sharing information that affects them in a timely, transparent way,
- trusting them until you have valid reasons not to,
- avoid encroaching on their desirable and sustainable work/life balance (or help them establish it),
- following through on promises made and honoring commitments,
- making sure work-related resources are commensurate and available for the work-related demands others face,
- modeling trust, honesty, keeping promises, respect for all, avoiding gossip, and speaking up for the powerless, and
- encouraging and supporting another's personal growth and learning.

Managers may not be able to honestly say "I love you" to everyone they work with, and that is okay. Sincerity and authenticity are vital. Yet, every manager can manage with a caring attitude. The most beloved managers are the ones who demonstrate care for their direct reports' well-being and sense of being known and valued. Consider the fact that "in four minutes, the turning earth moves one degree in longitude."[107] In four minutes, a world-class runner can run a mile. In four minutes, a manager can drop by a direct report's office and have a short, friendly, care-building conversation sparked by the simple words, "How are you doing?"

One week prior to the retirement celebration for my colleague, I had attended an elementary school graduation—fifth graders heading off to middle school the next year. The headmistress and a couple of the children spoke to the assembled parents, and they shared some funny stories. More significantly, they all spoke of their affection for the people they had spent time with that year, whether that was in the school's offices, classrooms, library, or playground. They knew each other and cared for each other. That week's bookend events caused me to think, *Why can't genuine care be a hallmark of our relationships with others for the years in between fifth grade and retirement?* No reason they can't be!

REFLECT: *When and how have you been cared for at work and outside work? What have you observed amongst and between others that have also been depictions of care? For any of these recollections, is there a sense of conviction or affirmation in your mind that you practice/exhibit them too? Why, and how? Do you know anybody who would not want to be on the receiving end of a caring attitude and care in action? Me neither.*

_____
_____
_____
_____

IDENTIFY: *In what specific ways can you extend or enhance the care you offer, display, and provide your direct reports? An old* *saying, applicable in this instance, is that actions speak louder than words. Be specific and realistic in identifying some caring things you can do more of or do better.*

_____
_____
_____
_____

SHARE: *Caution→ it is important to make sure that your action-oriented ideas for enhanced or extended care are not perceived by others as either a lack of confidence in them or trivial and condescending. Vet your care ideas with a colleague. Do they understand the value of enhanced and extended care to and for direct reports? Discuss this basic question with them. How much care is value-added versus counterproductive? Different manifestations of care for different people—yes or no? Are policies and guidelines for care warranted, or is it better to be serendipitous and idiosyncratic? Why? Please do not let the inability to find the perfect approach dilute or delay the possible.*

_____
_____
_____
_____

EVALUATE: *Care can be a core capability if you want it to be. Care will not diminish your standing with direct reports and colleagues, nor will it diminish your ability to manage or lead. If you have been a bit more proactive in extending and modeling care amongst your direct reports, after a few months, what reactions* *have you gotten? Do you feel different as a manager? If yes, in what way(s)? If not, why not? Care may not translate directly or immediately to improved organizational performance, but it will be a valued aspect of organizational culture and interpersonal relationships. Done well, broadly, and consistently, it may just lead to retirement farewell remarks that sincerely say, "I love each of you, and I love this place."*

... A FINAL CHAPTER 6 VIGNETTE ...

> **#36 Play an ACE as often as you can.**

*Our chief want is someone who will inspire us
to be what we know we could be.*[108]

—Ralph Waldo Emerson,
nineteenth-century iconic American poet and essayist

SEVERAL YEARS AGO, I experienced a first: a "change of command" ceremony for a high-ranking military friend at a nearby US Navy base. My friend, a man of faith devoted to family, was relinquishing his command of a test flight squadron and moving on to a new assignment at the Pentagon. It was a very warm and well-done occasion with a couple hundred people in attendance—civilians as well as other military members. Of course, the actual ceremony was patriotic, dignified, and inspirational, replete with numerous flags, a brass band, starched uniforms, respectful salutes, and impressive airplanes. For me, there was even more. As my friend and others spoke from the stage, I became aware of something that many of us seldom experience and do: the practice of playing an ACE.

The ceremony was a time of sincere *affirmation* (A) of others, an invitation to collectively *celebrate* (C) jobs well done, and an earnest offering of *encouragement* (E) for those who would be carrying on. *ACE* for short. Here, on an otherwise unremarkable rainy Thursday morning in a naval air station hangar, men and women of the US Navy and Marine Corps had declared a timeout; they had hit the pause button of their lives and work to celebrate and honor two of their own—the outgoing and the incoming commanders of the squadron.

Consider the simple task of *affirmation*. Work lives are so busy and becoming more and more virtual. Too often, managers motor right past countless opportunities to affirm those who work hard and do a good job every day. Yes, managers expect the people they hire to do their jobs and to do them well. However, why not acknowledge from time to time, for specific people, that they are seen, appreciated, and valued? The ones who are not the complainers, the ones who are not absent, the ones who always give assistance when asked, and the ones whose work is done on time and done well may not make headlines nor garner most of your attention, and yet, they are what we need. And nobody wants to be taken for granted. The workplace is a target-rich environment for affirmation opportunities—all the back-office people, customer service reps, administrative assistants, security guards providing directions from the front gate, external vendors of all types, and even third-party players such as auditors, regulators, and inspectors. A phone call, a short office visit, a mention in a newsletter, a callout in a group meeting—all simple things to convey the managerial message of "I see you. I appreciate what you do. Thank you!" I once mentioned to a group of managers that everyone deserves, during their life, at least one standing ovation for what they have done, who they have helped, or even just for the positive attitude they never fail to bring to work. At first, the remark was met with some skepticism by those in the audience, but by the end of our time together, many agreed with the spirit of the remark.

Celebration is a group activity with a focus on someone's or some group's contribution(s). Celebration spearheaded by one's manager builds esprit de corps, communicates an appreciation for valued accomplishment, and signals what all can contribute. Many years ago, the importance and significance of celebration were seared in my memory bank. I was doing some work for a regional ad agency. The agency was quite successful, had several national accounts, and employed several dozen professionals. Every Friday afternoon at about 3:30, all those in the building that day came out of their offices to a large, central communal space and broke out the refreshments—some of which were for adults only. It was their version of a happy hour, replete with senior manager toasts to individuals who performed outstandingly that week, went above and beyond the call of duty, or were instrumental in a significant accomplishment for the firm (e.g., landing a new client or winning an ad award). The cost to the firm for that hour and a half of "downtime," shared information, and celebration every Friday afternoon was recouped several times over in employee commitment to, affinity for, and effort for the agency. Clearly, happy hours are not the point—finding moments and means for celebrating is.

Encouragement is always appreciated by those receiving it. As I've emphasized, encouragement is best when linked with empowerment and enablement. And yet, there is also the role for an overarching encouragement that is more of the ilk of a rallying cry, a hands-in-the-middle, 1-2-3 let's go. Followers will follow when they see a trustworthy, enthusiastic manager providing tangible evidence of encouragement and sight lines to a desired destination. Management's words of encouragement can serve to reignite dedication, remind everyone of purpose and direction, and emphasize a need for one another.

Thinking back to my friend's change of command ceremony, I love the fact that those trained and dedicated to being fierce warriors for our nation unapologetically took the time to publicly affirm, celebrate, and encourage their own on that rainy Thursday morning. A Marine Corps general did so for my friend and those he had led. My friend, in turn, did the same for a number of those he had worked with and was leaving behind. Likewise, the newly appointed commander did the same for those who had helped him reach this command point in his career. As a stone thrown into a pond produces an ever-expanding array of ripples that fall onto many points along the shoreline, my friend's change of command ceremony was a time of rippling affirmations, celebrations, and encouragements—those in the spotlight each played an *ACE*.

REFLECT: *Quietly spend the next week looking for prime moments for playing a quiet, one-on-one ACE or a moment that would warrant a wider public display. Make note of those moments and occasions. Look for those moments and occasions internally, up and down, and across the organization as well as externally. It might be some very subtle things that catch your eye, such as someone overcoming a significant challenge or setback, someone selflessly sharing information and insights with new hires, someone taking the initiative to tackle a recurring problem, or someone covering for a coworker who had to minister to an ill dependent at home all week. Opportunities to "play an ACE" are more frequent than we might have thought.*

_____

_____

_____

_____

IDENTIFY: *What four or five opportunities for playing an ACE did you identify? What formal or informal ways can you envision playing an ACE for each of those instances? How and when should you play an ACE so that it never becomes a devalued, routinized ritual? Have you ever stood up in a meeting and initiated a standing ovation for a colleague for something they had done that many others may not have known about? When exceptionally warranted, try it; it will be a profound moment for that person, for you, and for those watching. Doing* *so is akin to a pause, with full eye contact and erect posture, raising a slow and lingering salute from one person to another, regardless of rank.*

_____
_____
_____
_____

SHARE: *If you perceive that your organization at large and/or your department is somewhat remiss in playing an ACE from time to time, share that observation with a colleague. Do they agree, and why or why not? Do you still believe it to be true within the realm(s) in which you operate at work? If so, share with your colleague the idea(s) you are formulating to change that situation. Use their comments to fine-tune yours for when and how to play an ACE. (I would like to suggest that the "when" not simply be at a retirement event.)*

_____
_____
_____
_____

EVALUATE: *How has your playing an ACE been received by colleagues, direct reports, and especially those for whom the ACE was aimed? Were you disappointed, pleased, and/or surprised by the reactions you got? Why or why not? What heretofore uncelebrated sorts of contributions can now be spotlighted and receive an ACE? Think broadly and creatively, as this is an opportunity for championing intangibles, the selfless actions often taken for* *granted that foster collaboration, preserve organizational values, and establish foundations for future success.*

CHAPTER 7
Find Your Virtuous Cycle

WE HAVE ALL heard of, if not experienced, the travails of a vicious cycle. For example, you sleep through your alarm, arrive late at the airport, miss your flight, reroute your travel itinerary, and arrive late at that night's rehearsal dinner for your best friend. Or, you are late on a deliverable, which makes the next one late also, affecting others and creating an error-prone rush to get it all done. What has hopefully happened for you from this book, however, is not another vicious cycle but rather a virtuous one. A cycle where one insight leads to an idea, which leads to a commitment to action, which leads to positive change that fuels the desire for another new insight and so on.

Some of the cues for reflection presented for you here were probably more meaningful or timelier than others. Why was that? Was it because some seemed more difficult to operationalize while others did not? Was it because you thought you needed the potential benefits from this one more than that one? Go back to what you passed over or set aside and challenge the rationale that sparked that.

"Hot Wash"—Your After-Action Review

In the military, an after-action review is often prepared on an operation, sometimes called a Hot Wash. A Hot Wash is worthwhile for any of the vignettes for which you crafted and pursued an idea for action. Take some time, perhaps a day or a week, and then return to that vignette and your responses to it to consider again how it went, what you learned, what you would do differently, and why. In my own experience and in probing other managers to dig a bit deeper into their own learning, there is always a bit more to be gleaned, a bit more to become crystallized, and a bit more to commit to doing. Tap that vein of gold for all it has.

Your "experiment" is not complete until you do the Hot Wash. Document each vignette's personal actions as if it were an after-action review. Then, set it aside for several months or a year. Let them stack up. Then, revisit them. See if there is a galvanizing 2.0 version that occurs for you—a renewed and repeated process for initiating a virtuous learning cycle of reflection → identify an idea → sharing → evaluating (i.e., **RISE**).

Become a Galvanizer!

"Learning organizations" learn because individuals take action to preserve and share important lessons they have acquired that improve the organization. Scale and scope do not matter. It is worthwhile to preserve and share lessons learned with even just one other person. Consider being a teacher, formal or informal, within the organization so that the lessons you have learned from this endeavor are preserved and extended to others. Be open to the possibility that others may need to modify a lesson you present to them for it to fit their context, their history, their responsibilities, and their goals. That is okay. The core element of any important lesson can take on a variety of manifestations.

If you find yourself fortunate enough to have a colleague who is intrigued by how you invested in your own managerial development using this book, feel free to recommend it to them. More importantly, feel free to volunteer to them that you would be honored to serve as the trusted colleague with whom they can share raw ideas for discussion, reaction, and refinement for their managerial development.

Capstone Codification

I have never kept a diary. I do not have the discipline to do so. I have, however, throughout my career, kept a running set of notes on things accomplished and projects to consider doing. The former was input to my annual performance review report. The latter captured an array of intriguing ideas that I frequently referred to when one project ended and I was deciding on what endeavor to pursue next. May I suggest that you do both too? The former to document your MQp growth and development worthy of your own celebration. The latter so that you are reminded of the continuous nature of development, rife with lots of rich and intriguing avenues to pursue.

I will also confess that whenever I read my list of possible job-related project to-dos, just the length and variety of it excites me and reminds me of the multifaceted nature of the opportunities that potentially await my focus, my efforts, and my talents. The energy and excitement necessary for a productive forty-year career must come from somewhere. For me, it came mostly from identifying numerous possibilities for collaborating with others. Perhaps that, too, can, in some measure, fuel the remaining best years of your forty-year management career. All the best!

BONUS MATERIAL
DIY (Do-It-Yourself)
Home Improvement Project Parallels

BESIDES FAITH, FAMILY, AND FRIENDS, one of the biggest pleasures in my life is having a rewarding vocation as well as an enjoyable avocation. Most weekends and many evenings, I'm engaged in a DIY home improvement project. Such endeavors can be quite varied. They often require creative problem-solving since I am not a pro at that sort of thing. Enjoyably, such projects necessitate an ever-growing inventory of fun tools, they generally end with observable results, and occasionally, they involve a friend's helping hand. Over the years, what has been fascinating to me are the parallels that emerge between the principles of management that I most value and the insights that guided me on a particular DIY project. Digging deeper into those connections has also revealed lessons learned from one arena that can be applied to the other—a fun, symbiotic relationship. If two disparate fields are appealing to you, chances are that it is the commonality of attributes resident in each that are the primary attraction. That has been true for me.

Perhaps there is a connectivity of vocation and avocation for you. I can think of three friends who are passionate about their avocations, and they see parallels between them and certain aspects of management. One of those friends spends much of his nonwork, nonfamily time engaged with restoring and touring with others in their vintage cars. Another friend is avid about traditional golf and classic hickory golf. The third friend is a wonderful amateur chef. What is your avocation? What do you like about it, and why? What are the subtleties and nuances of it that have management parallels for you?

This book was born on a family vacation when my kids were little. There was lots of car time and, fortunately, lots of quiet time as the kids read, slept, played video games, or listened to music. That is when my mind started its own journey, making vocation/avocation connections. It was fun. It became my mental gymnasium while rolling down the highway. As the connections mounted, I had to involve my wife for fear of forgetting what I had tentatively teed up in my thinking as a connection based on a remembrance of an exemplifying event. She graciously became my notetaker, writing down random words that would later cue me but didn't mean much to her.

I highly recommend a session or two at the mental gym! When you have the luxury of letting your mind wander, see if you can come up with five nuggets from your avocation and make a valid connection to an insight pertaining to your managerial vocation. If that comes easily and quickly, see if you can come up with five more, and so on. You might be pleasantly surprised by the numerous parallels or connections.

Here are some from my DIY world. The numbered heading shown for each vignette below corresponds to the management vignette used earlier. Below it is the parallel DIY heading, followed by a personal DIY vignette for your enjoyment. These DIY insights are not needed to support or flesh out any of the earlier management insights they are linked to—those earlier lessons are valid on a stand-alone basis. Perhaps the ensuing avocational connections might spur you to make your own. Moreover, if you are also a DIY home improvement person, you might be able to relate to many of these, and you may also have your own that complement or better substitute for what I share. Enjoy!

> **#1 *Fast track. Sidetrack. Backtrack. Off track. Best track.***
>
>  DIY
>
> *Find a fast-track method and avoid the backtrack.*

In custom-built sheds, garages, houses, and cabins, gabled roof rafters can present a modest challenge. Each rafter requires several cuts—an angled cut at the top, a notch near the other end to sit on the wall plate, and then a squared-off end to accept fascia and soffit boards. One way to do each rafter is to measure and mark the locations for each of the needed cuts. One mismeasurement and mismarking on the rafter board will render the cuts wrong and necessitate backtracking and redoing, possibly discarding that potential rafter board and moving on to an entirely new one. The most reliable way to keep a project on track is to carefully measure, mark, and cut one rafter. Make sure it fits as needed at several points along the center ridge beam and the wall's top plate, and then clearly designate it as the rafter template. Then, all the other rafters can be accurately and quickly marked by simply tracing the outline of the cuts to be made using that template rafter. A fast, efficient, reliable way.

Templates are a perfect way to proceed when your project involves multiples of any component part of what you are building. Stair stringers, window boxes, shudders, on-site-built parquet flooring, and anything with round (complete or partial) cuts are examples of when a template can be used to stay on the fast track and avoid the backtrack.

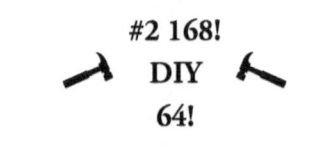

#2 168! DIY 64!

Firepits are an enjoyable gathering place, especially on cool evenings. A ready supply of neatly stacked firewood eliminates some of the chore of the endeavor. I needed a handy stack of dry firewood, but I did not need a full cord of wood. A cord of wood is 128 cubic feet. I decided to build a storage rack for half a cord of wood—64 cubic feet. I needed some two-by-fours for the frame and some one-by-eights for the bottom. I wanted it to be strong and simple. To hold a half-cord of firewood, it needed to be eight feet long, two feet deep, and four feet high (8 x 4 x 2 = 64). I am always keen for a bit of a challenge, so the fun aspect of building it was to do so with no wasted material. How many two-by-fours and one-by-eights did I need such that every inch of what I bought was used? With some quick figuring, here was my shopping list:

- five two-by-fours, eight feet long,
- one two-by-four, twelve feet long, and
- two one-by-eights, twelve feet long.

I built it. I had no boards left over. Success. I use that rack to this day. A scarce resource (boards) used wisely can produce valuable results.

Just in case you are curious, the front view of one end is depicted below. Part A is a four-foot upright (four of those). Each paired four-foot upright is topped and bottomed with a two-foot board connecting them (the darkened part in the diagram). Part B is an eight-foot horizontal piece (two of those) with a two-foot cap at both ends connecting the long, eight-foot paired boards. Part B is also plated on its top side with minimally spaced two-foot sections of one-by-eight (not shown in diagram). The diagonal is a two-foot piece of two-by-four lumber; there are four of those diagonals to strengthen the uprights at each end of the rack. Simple and strong and a precise use of materials planned and purchased.

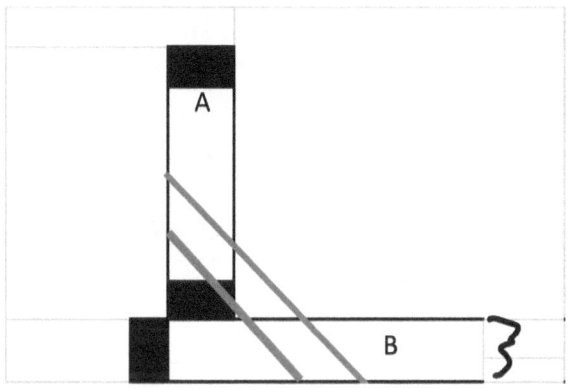

#3 *Different management executives fail in amazingly similar ways.*

 DIY

DIYers have all failed in similar ways.

Most, if not all, DIYers have made the same mistakes in their journey to becoming competent DIYers. Those mistakes are seldom costly in any significant or lasting way, but they can be annoying and project-delaying. The DIY Hall of Fame Mistakes that beginners often encounter and veterans wryly smile about include:

- failing to measure twice when you can only cut once, thus wasting a board cut too short,
- failing to sand a tabletop thoroughly to get a perfectly smooth finish,
- failing to reduce the torque when driving a screw, snapping it in half,
- failing to use a nail set tool, leaving a hammer-head-sized dent

on the wood,
- failing to hit the nail with the hammer and instead squarely hitting your thumb,
- failing to wear eye protection and getting a splinter in the eye,
- failing to sharpen the saw's teeth, thus causing it to needlessly bind when in use,
- failing to carefully watch your step on a ladder and falling, and
- failing to put a drop cloth under an item being painted, and paint ends up on the floor.

I'm sure there are many other misadventures that cause experienced DIYers to both roll their eyes and nod their heads when newbies confess to having done them. The point is that the gray-haired DIYers have extracted lessons from such failures and avoid making the same mistake again. (For example, I will measure twice before sawing. I will be patient and meticulous when I am sanding. I will hang the safety glasses next to the table saw so I am reminded to wear them. I will use a drop cloth under the ladder when I am painting.) Beginning DIYers often don't think such simple mistakes will happen to them. And yet, one day, they will.

#4 *Seize the binding benefits of residential management development programs.*

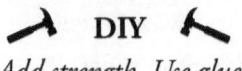 DIY

Add strength. Use glue.

The clerk at the home improvement store said I should glue down the new subflooring I was installing in my attic conversion home theater project. He said it would preempt a squeaky floor and create a stronger, more stable flooring system. I dutifully bought several big tubes of construction adhesive and a biggiesized caulking gun for applying it. There was a real sense of "doing it like the pros" as one sheet of glued subflooring went down and then another and then another. I was flying and feeling very purposeful. As I cleaned up my mess at the end of the day, there was no doubt that it had been a good day.

Glue bonds two pieces of wood by penetrating the surfaces of the two boards and then drying. Thus, the hardened glue does not merely exist between the two boards; it becomes a part of them. If the means for separating the two boards is to try and pull or pry them apart, the wood grain will give way before the glued seam. A glued joint can't be broken once it has been allowed to set. That floor neither flexes nor squeaks.

#5 Locate, legitimate, liberate, and love leverage.

 DIY

With leverage, one can do the work of two.

They were a bargain, so I bought them. I would eventually need some. The purchase was one of those in-the-ceiling pull-down attic stairs. I could barely carry them from the driveway to the site of the attic remodeling project that was underway. They were heavy! How was I going to hoist them up into the room's ceiling joists? I knew that if I could rest them on top of those joists, I could then nail a couple of boards underneath onto two adjoining joists and lower the folding stairs unit onto those temporary cross boards so that I could then bolt it through its two sides into the joists once it was in its final position.

But how was I going to get such a heavy object eight feet up above the ceiling joists all by myself? It finally dawned on me that if I took a long length of a two-by-eight or two-by-six board, I could lean that board against the top edge of a ceiling joist and use it as a ramp from the floor. I could then push the stair unit up that ramp. It worked like a charm. That incline made it possible for me, all alone, to leverage my limited strength to get something that weighed more than I could lift to a height of eight feet and in place for bolting to the two joists it was to sit between. I was so proud of that solution. I was also quite pleased that I had not had to call my wife for help. I called out to her anyway to come see what I had so ingeniously figured out in sparing her the dreaded request—"Honey, could you help me for a moment?"

> #6 *Be a bridge. Connect others. Connect functions. Connect processes.*
>
>  DIY
>
> *Without excellent design, great execution is wasted. Without excellent execution, great design is wasted. Connect the two.*

The month of March always calls me to start an outside project. That March, it was a self-designed, built-in bench for the deck. It was more than a bench in that it had a back and arms and was about six feet long. With a light breeze, late afternoon shade, and cold beer, the bench was going to look great and feel great with some of those big pillowy cushions that can be purchased at any discount chain store.

I approached building the bench with great care and meticulousness. Once it was built, I stood back to admire it. Something didn't look right. After several days of staring at it, it dawned on me that the supports holding it up and connecting it to the deck were undersized for the mass of the bench itself. It looked like a sofa resting on toothpicks. The solution was simple: nail extra widths of lumber on either side of both supports to simply beef them up. The carpentry on the original design was good, but the original design was not. I needed the bench to connect to the deck in an aesthetically appealing way.

Another part of the calendar also calls to me. The month of January always makes me feel claustrophobic and antsy. I needed an inside project, and I had the perfect one. Two years earlier, my wife had requested a grandfather clock for an anniversary present. In frugal acquiescence, I had bought a kit, and it was now time to assemble it. The 100 or so cherrywood pieces were beautiful, finely cut, and flawless. The clock went together with an appropriate amount of challenge to make it enjoyable and with enough ease to make it doable. It was finally assembled, and my wife had already cleared the wall space where it was to stand. All that was left for me to do was apply the stain and clearcoat finish. I dreaded that part, and sure enough, I messed it up big time. It turned out blotchy and plain ugly. Only one viable remedy. I called an antique restoration guy and pleaded, "Help!" He came and got it, quoted me a price I was all too happy to pay, and took it away. The clock came back two weeks later and looked marvelous. I am not sure how he rescued it. Without his aid, I would have precisely assembled a clock of great design, but its beauty would have been severely compromised because I had executed the finishing of it—the very final stage—so badly. Quality assembly and quality finish needed to be connected. That clock still chimes on the hour in our living room.

#7 Hope and osmosis.

🔨 DIY 🔨

Hope and osmosis 2.0.

Osmosis does not work. When I was a young boy, my dad often drafted me to be his unpaid, close-at-hand, Saturday morning home improvement helper. It wasn't every Saturday morning, but it was a lot of them. I don't remember them very fondly. The biggest problem was that even though he was good at what he was tackling, he was not particularly patient or prone to teaching. On the contrary, it seemed to me that he assumed I knew what to do when he called for this or that, asked me to do this or that, or wanted me to make the appropriate adjustment to this or that. I often did not know what the "this and the that" were the first time around. It seemed that he thought I understood what needed to be done by simply seeing a particular circumstance unfold as he undertook his tasks. I'm sure he wished my assistance would have been immediate and just what he needed. But there was no osmosis flowing from him to me during any of the projects that I was drafted into. I needed him to pause, show, explain, and do so again if necessary. He had lots of capabilities—timely and patient instruction was not always one of them.

I am guilty of being overly hopeful in many of my projects, especially when I am in a hurry or dislike a particular part of a project and want it to be done. I implicitly hope good enough is actually good enough, or I hope that the skipped step won't really matter. Normally, those situations arise during the final phases of a project. For example, I have often failed to do a thorough job of sanding, wiping clean, sanding again, and wiping clean again a tabletop or shelf that I have just made or am refinishing. Oh, what about those slight blemishes in the wood or that small patch of roughness? In response, I tell myself, "The paint or varnish will smooth that out." That is wishful thinking. That is a hope not supported by any prior experiences, just a raw hope arising because I am in a hurry and ready to move on to the next project. I have since learned to hire someone to do the finish work on my projects from time to time because I know my thinking at that stage of a project is usually something like: "That shortcut is okay . . . It won't matter . . . No one will notice . . . It will be fine . . . I need to be finished with it." Nope, such hope seldom works out.

> **#8 *Have a freedom fund.***
>
>  DIY
>
> *A financial cushion can be quite helpful.*

Even though I have been blessed with a steady job and a good income, I have been house-poor at times. Too big of a mortgage results in too many sleepless nights worrying about it. Several years ago, such sleepless nights motivated me to take action to remedy the situation—sell the big house, pay off the big mortgage, and buy a smaller house with a smaller mortgage. In so doing, I was able to build up some financial cushion after having been stretched financially for too long.

The beauty of that resulting cushion was twofold. First, I could pay cash for ensuing projects and not have to accumulate credit card debt. That felt good. And I learned that many subcontractors are willing to discount their quotes if your payments to them are in cash. I've saved 7 to 10 percent on original estimates by offering to pay cash. Second, and somewhat unexpectedly, I was able to be more compassionate when a deal broke down. More specifically, a contractor quit on me after I had advanced him some money on a big project (big for me, at least). A few months later, I got a registered government letter in the mail notifying me that he had filed for bankruptcy, and I had a certain amount of time to note for the court any financial claims that I believed I was entitled to. My wife and I thought about what to do for a couple of weeks. He owed us a couple thousand dollars for work he had not done. But we also felt compassion for him. According to his son, whom we got to know, this middle-aged contractor was financially ruined, with no new prospects, and he had sunk into a deep depression. Since my wife and I had established a little financial cushion, we decided not to submit any claims. Why pour more salt on a wound that was already very painful for that person? We felt we did the right thing.

> **#9 Focus on focus.**
>  DIY
> *It's important to know what you don't know as well as knowing that plumbers don't do electrical or carpentry and vice versa.*

I was running behind schedule on the bathroom that was part of a finish-the-basement project. The plumber was scheduled to come on Tuesday to rough in the drainpipes and water lines for the shower, toilet, and sink. The shower, however, posed a mild departure from the norm. The basement floor was a concrete slab, and I was not about to tear it up for a shower drain that I had quite intentionally positioned about three feet from where the original builder had pre-positioned a drain in the slab. Thus, the shower required a slightly raised platform under which the drainpipe could run across the top of the concrete floor to the existing in-slab drain three feet away. Well, I hadn't quite gotten around to building the platform before Tuesday. I figured that since the plumber was going to be there, he could help me build the platform, and then he could do his thing. Wrong! You would think that I asked him to engage in a criminal act. There was no way he was going to do any carpentry. He would wait and charge me while he waited for me to build the platform. That is exactly what I did and exactly what he did.

In another instance, I had ordered a couple of yards of concrete for a small patio behind our house. There was no way to get the cement truck back there, so I knew the cement would have to be wheelbarrowed from the front of the house. When the truck arrived, I had two wheelbarrows ready to go and suggested that the unloading of the concrete would go faster if the driver took one of the wheelbarrows and helped. Now, I grant you that such work is not the easiest, nor a task many people would volunteer to do. The driver of the truck was almost surly in his refusal to help. His job was to simply drive the truck and open/close the spigot from which the concrete poured—after that, I was on my own.

If a bedroom needs a bigger closet, I can build it. If a sunroom needs ceramic tile, I can install it. If it is time for a new hot water heater, however, I call my plumber. If a three-way electrical switch needs to be added in the living room, I call my electrician. If two fifty-foot-high trees in the yard need to be taken down, I call Barry, the logger. If three skylights need to be installed in my 12/12 pitched roof, I call my builder. I know the limits of my capabilities and my level of interest (or lack of interest) in learning others. I have a contacts list with the phone numbers of some high-quality, reasonably priced, reliable tradespeople who can do what I cannot or do not want to do. Moreover, these tradespeople know that they are my person of choice when I need assistance and are thus very willing to take care of me when I give them a call. It is not all good news, however. I am still trying to find an appliance repair person that I can rely on—the last one I scheduled never came.

#10 *Paint the picture.*

If I can picture it, I can usually build it.

The landscape architect said that a large gazebo or pergola would look great right there. Indeed, I agreed and put it on my DIY to-do list. You must understand that many items stay on that list forever, while others are there only a few years, and others get immediate attention. The gazebo fell into the middle category. Over the years, as I thought about the gazebo, I knew that I didn't want one of those small, cutesy, delicately trimmed Victorian structures with a style like those that can be bought ready-made at large home center stores. What was taking rough shape in my mind's eye was something more like a small outdoor pavilion (e.g., fourteen feet square).

Unexpectedly, it happened on a winter's Sunday afternoon. I had just taken my son to his indoor soccer game, and since it was unseasonably warm and sunny, I decided to walk around the neighborhood where the gym was located while I waited for his game to start. There it was . . . exactly what I wanted to build . . . in someone else's backyard. It was perfect in every way. I had seen it! My foggy mental image had been brought into sharp focus. It was now in my mind's eye (plus, I had a couple of hastily taken pictures for added ease of recollection). It would now be quite buildable. I had hoped to have the structure finished in time for my daughter's wedding. I didn't. It did, however, get done a few years later in time for my son's wedding.

#11 *Learn from "stay interviews."*
🔨 DIY 🔨
Passionate DIYers engage all their senses and come back for more.

I am pleasantly cursed in my home-improvement carpentry of being a hedonist. Take a simple interaction with a two-by-four piece of lumber to be used in framing a door. First, there is the lengthwise sighting of several candidates from the storage pile for the one that is perfectly straight. Next is the measuring, marking, and even the pleasant thought that this board will contribute to the overall goal of creating a doorway that will provide both access and privacy. Then comes the act of sawing the board, with the sound of power in my hand progressively cutting along the line. Next, there is the satisfying feel of running my hand across the fresh cut to swipe away small splinters and gauge its smoothness. For me, it is then impossible to resist the desire to hold the cut end of the board to my nose to smell the fragrance of the freshly exposed grain. In then placing the board in the position for which it was intended, there is a moment's pleasure in seeing its tight, flush fit. Next comes the nailing of the board in its place and the real awareness that this is permanent, this is final, this is purposeful. Then, there is the stepping back and looking at the in-place two-by-four and appreciating one more tangible bit of progress. Finally, let your mouth taste the cold drink at the end of a productive DIY-project day and enjoy its punctuating satisfaction. Why have five senses, five different ways to enjoy what you do, and not use them all? I use them, and that is why I keep doing such projects. Is gardening your passion? Acknowledge the same sensory appreciation to each aspect of those DIY projects—the soil, the plants, the mulch, the fertilizer, the water, and the landscape bricks or timbers. If you enjoy all such aspects and ingredients of your DIY tasks, why move on to golf? Stay with DIY.

> **#12 *One bad constituent-facing employee encounter can ruin a relationship.***
>
>  DIY
>
> *One bad bearing in a floor sander can ruin a floor.*

Cherrywood is magnificent. It is rich, warm, and varied in its hues, tones, and grain. One of the design features of the first house we built was that the hardwood floors were random-width cherry. They were beautiful. The path to the finished result, however, was not without anguish and disappointment. The cherry flooring was installed right on time, and we booked the floor finishing team to come in on a Saturday. It was a father-and-son duo. By the end of Sunday, it was to be only a matter of letting the floor finish cure for a couple of days before we could walk on it and complete the few remaining tasks prior to movein day. To their credit, I got a call on Monday from the duo asking me to meet them at the house after work. All day, I wondered what was up. When I got there, they pointed out how the semigloss floor finish applied the day before, and now dry, brought to their attention some very noticeable grooves running the length of the floor. Their big, powerful floor sander had done the damage, and they wanted to redo the floor. Of course, they would do it all over again, at no extra charge, and they would do it immediately so as not to create any additional project delay. They began again that night.

To this day, there are still places where the floor is not perfectly smooth, and if I let myself, I can still get a little upset about that. The cause was a bad bearing in their power sander that made the sanding drum spin with an eversoslight shimmy, thus creating a small but continuous and noticeable groove every eight inches or so as they progressively moved back and forth across the room. The two men were pros, their approach was correct, and their part of the execution was fine. It all failed because one element in the overall process was not operating at the required level of excellence.

#13 *20/80 or 80/20?*
➔ DIY ✎
The last 20% accounts for 80% of the final look.

Our new sunroom was going to be spectacular. It was elevated about ten feet above ground, replete with lots of full-length windows, and it faced the hardwood forest only thirty feet away. That last weekend in October, we found ourselves two months and thousands of dollars into the project. Everything was done except for the finished flooring and painting. Early that Saturday morning, we knew the end was in sight, but at that moment, the room still had a very unfinished, in-process, construction-site look to it.

Not for long! That weekend, my wife and I and another couple primed the walls and ceiling and laid down a beautiful ceramic tile floor. In a matter of two days, and for only several hundred dollars, the room was virtually finished and had taken on the look of a *House Beautiful,* come-spend-quality-time-in-me sunroom. The same phenomenon occurs when a room is wallpapered or an antique dresser is given a new coat of stain and lacquer after a laborious stripping and repairing phase. Those last few steps are usually eagerly anticipated and always crucial to the successful, satisfying completion of the project. It doesn't matter how strong the floor framing is if the tile is laid crooked. It doesn't matter how nice the bathroom fixtures are if the wallpaper pattern is misaligned. It doesn't matter how carefully the loose joinery on an antique dresser is repaired if the wet lacquer is allowed to run and collect dust. The last 20 percent of the project accounts for 80 percent (or more) of the final look and requires 100 percent of your attention.

#14 *Regularly perform an assumptions audit.*
DIY
Validate and question assumptions.

In an adult lifetime of DIY projects, I've learned to take nothing for granted. For example, hanging wallpaper in a turn-of-the-century home may seem straightforward, but it is frequently problematic. What appear to be square and straight corners aren't, and that striped wallpaper you chose for the hallway will accentuate every non-square corner. Another example, do you like to do a little electrical wiring job occasionally? Then you know never to assume the power has been turned off until *you* have checked the electrical panel.

Even when you think it is safe to assume something, be very sure. In a house we recently built, the two-by-ten band board the contractor had lag-screwed to the house seemed sufficient for attaching a deck. When the county inspector looked at it, he remembered the floor system in the house was composed of webbed trusses, not dimensional-lumber joists. He wondered out loud if the band board's lag screws had been positioned to penetrate some of the truss structure or simply lag-screwed into the half-inch sheathing covering the ends of the floor trusses. He asked me to remove a couple of lag screws to find out. Sure enough, the contractor had not bothered to drive lag screws into the substantive parts of the truss framing. Nor had he used sufficiently long lag screws. Fortunately, the inspector had sought to verify what, in most instances, would have been a legitimate assumption. So, I had to redo the entire band board's attachments . . . probing for, finding enough truss structure to reposition about twenty longer lag screws. Thank goodness for that inspector. I would have wrongly assumed the band board was suitable for the deck.

#15 *Subject your KPIs to a behavioral audit.*
🔨 DIY 🔨
When building, keep checking the bubble.

The framing crew at our house was impressive from the beginning. I arrived at the jobsite one afternoon to see three of them, down on their knees, with eight-foot-long levels, checking the first floor's joists in all directions. The question driving this checking and rechecking was "Are the tops of the floor joists perfectly level with one another in all directions?" In those spots where the joists weren't, they planed them a little so that they were. Such a check provided assurance that in the future, the vintage Virginia merlot I served my guests would rest level in the wine decanter that sat on the table, that stood on the finished floor, that rested on the subfloor, that had been built on top of a perfectly level array of floor joists.

A level is one of the most elegantly simple and reliable tools that has ever been invented. It is easy to use and interpret. The level is a tool that has proven its usefulness for centuries and whose sole purpose is to monitor only two conditions—whether something is perfectly horizontal (e.g., leveling floor joists) and whether something is perfectly vertical (e.g., making a wall vertical). If a construction component is not level (i.e., horizontal) or plumb (i.e., vertical), the other elements of the project will subsequently not fit nor function properly, and the finished look of the job will not be pleasing to the eye. When building, there is a critical rule—keep checking the bubble in a level to make sure it is okay to continue or to pause and make adjustments to get the outcomes desired.

#16 *Ask hard questions even when receiving good financial news.*
🔨 DIY 🔨
Ask hard questions of the low bidder.

Whenever possible, I try to get at least two bids for the parts of a project I plan to subcontract to a pro. Historically, I have been drawn to the "low-bid wins." That is no longer my automatic default move because that has not always worked out well. Yes, the low bid looks attractive, maybe even several thousand dollars less than the next closest one. But I've learned (the hard way at times) that I did not ask all the right questions, things like:

- Where do you buy your materials, and are they top-of-the-line?
- Are the workers you use your full-time employees or part-timers used only periodically?
- What are the dollar breakdowns in your bid for materials, labor, and profit?
- How long do you project the job will take, and are such projections reliable?
- Your bid price is quite different from your competitor's. Why?

Such basic questions are intended to provide insights regarding an approach to quality, operating practices, the reasonableness of profit margin, and the existence (or not) of the financial pressure a contractor is taking on if I hire them. In the past, I have had a low-bid contractor quit on me because halfway through a project, he determined he could not finish it profitably! On another occasion, I had to fire a low-bid subcontractor for their crew's unsightly work—that "crew" being a group of day laborers they had hired that morning at the local labor union hall. In another instance, I had to redo some shoddy work that came to light only after the low-bid subcontractor had been paid and left. Similarly, I have had to upgrade materials that a subcontractor used because those materials looked terrible after just a few years. All these situations arose in part because I accepted the low bid and did not ask some simple, probing questions.

Now, let it be said that I have benefitted from getting multiple bids and accepting the low one after asking some of those probing questions. I can think of a painter I hired who was half the cost of another, and he did a fine job. I think the other painter either didn't really want the job or wanted to price-gouge me. I can think of a framer whose cost was 30 percent lower than the next closest bid I received. He did great work, and I hired him after my due diligence questions. I determined he had a small company with much less overhead than the other bidder and was able to price his work lower. Just because a bid is lower does not make it better. Nor does it make it worse. Your task is to ask probing, key, follow-on questions before saying, "The job is yours."

#17 *Resolve and value disagreements.*
🔨 DIY 🔨
Two different tools can sometimes simultaneously achieve a single objective.

When I was eight or nine, my dad spent the better part of a year finishing our basement into a bedroom, bathroom, playroom, laundry room, and a shop for all his tools. I don't remember being too interested until I learned that the bedroom was going to be mine. Suddenly, I was curious about what was inside the wall and above the ceiling, as well as how a switch on one side of the room turned on a light across the room. I started hanging around down there as he worked, but I was too small to be of much help except for responding to the occasional, "Hand me that hammer, please, Son." One thing I do clearly remember was the odd way my dad hammered a nail (this was before nail guns existed) during the framing stage of carpentry—he held the nail with a pair of pliers and then hammered it. I asked why he did that since every other time I had seen a nail hammered, it did not involve a pair of pliers. The answer was that because he was using Douglas fir framing lumber, a board much denser and harder than the common white pine lumber more frequently used for framing walls, the pliers helped keep the nail stout and straight. As I have learned firsthand, nails tend to bend in hard lumber unless you can squarely strike the head every time. By squarely, I mean perfectly square. Thus, he showed me how two very different tools, used in concert with one another, helped achieve the simple objective of a nailed board when using dense/hard lumber. (I have also found this technique helpful when pounding in a nail that you previously bent, straightened, and are reusing.)

Another useful example. In extracting nails involving a sheetrock surface or a finely finished piece of wood, two disparate tools can again be effectively used to accomplish the task without marring/denting the surrounding surface. A claw hammer and a wide putty knife are the perfect combination in that situation. The putty knife, placed between the hammer's prying point and the surrounding surface, protects that surface and allows the hammer to do its work. Envisioning how two disparate tools can be combined for one special task is an instinct developed over time, prompted by a problem needing to be solved, producing pleasing and better results.

> **#18 *See over the horizon.***
> ➤ DIY ➤
> *Envision its use before you build it.*

When building a house, remodeling one, or making an addition to one, there is an important task that best precedes final construction plans. That task is giving conscientious thought to how you want to use that space once it is finished. The answer(s) to that question will guide parts of the design and build. For example, we were building a house in the woods . . . no neighbors nearby. I envisioned a bathtub soak at the end of a long afternoon of yard work, looking out the window into the nearby beautiful woods. From that vision came the realization that installing a casement window that could be cranked open at the tub-top level would create the feel of an indoor hot tub in the woods. We did that. It was great.

Similarly, we knew we would want an upper-level family room. At the time of construction, we didn't know what sorts of details we might want in it or when we would need it. We wanted a blank canvas. We asked the builder to stick-build the roof system instead of using trusses. The former would maximize the unobstructed space in what could then become an attic family room. We also asked the HVAC contractor to run all the ducts along the perimeter of that space, again preserving open floor space for future use. They did. It remained as an attic—only a potential living space—until six years later, when we easily finished the space into a multimedia room.

Looking at the plans for another house we were building, it struck us that an exterior, alcove corner off the master bedroom would make an ideal spot for a private deck with built-in planters. There was no time to design it and get a change order executed. The solution to keep the project moving was for the builder to add an exterior door in that corner of the bedroom (blocking it off on the outside) and to install and flash exterior ledger boards from which I could eventually build the deck. He did. Six years later, I did.

I firmly believe that for home construction and remodels, anticipated use informs design, not vice versa. To anticipate use requires envisioning the future: What do you plan to do in that space? What do you want it to feel like when using it? What are the most enjoyable outward sight lines to preserve? What do you want near that space and in that space? Time spent on such questions will increase the odds that you will love the result.

#19 *Prototype to accelerate the process.*
🔨 **DIY** 🔨
If unsure, build a mockup.

They were big, heavy, eight-foot-long, six-by-six pieces of pressure-treated lumber. In my eyes, though, they were future farm gate posts, with decoratively cut tops, targeted for an opening to a beautiful fifteen-acre parcel of meadow with a branch of Ivy Creek running through it. With a table saw, I knew it would be possible to make some angled cuts to give the top a wraparound V-groove that sat at the bottom of a gracefully tapered top. What I wasn't sure of were the proportions of the groove or the tapered top. The final look of the post had to appeal to my sense of proportionality as well as the scrutiny of my neighbors.

I had a scrap three-foot length of the same size lumber. I experimented with ever more angled, ever wider cuts and tapers and grooves, standing back from it each time to simply see if the proportions looked good to my eye. After a series of such progressive cuts, I had a prototype of the top two feet of the final farm gate posts that looked pleasing and was doable with the tools I had. All that was left was to transfer the lines of the mockup to the actual, larger two posts and make the cuts. I am happy to report that the final posts look great, and to this day, they continue to elegantly, but simply announce the entrance to the meadow tucked behind that house.

#20 *LBM—Let go. Back off. Move over.*
➤ DIY ➤
LBM—Leave it be. Better not. Motor on.

It was our first home—a 1920s four-over-four house. It had potential, and my wife and I were young and ready to tackle its remodeling. One of the first things we decided to do was strip the wallpaper off the upstairs master bedroom ceiling. Perhaps ceiling wallpaper was all the rage during some past decade, but it wasn't any longer. We rented a steamer and dove in early one Saturday morning in July. We were rookies, and we tended to do the ready, fire, aim version of planning and work. First, we discovered that there were three layers of wallpaper on the ceiling, not just one. This was going to take a while. Second, and we should have known this, the ceiling was made of plaster on lathe, not some early version of sheetrock. Well, that would beneficially give us a harder surface on which we could scrape the wallpaper off without worrying about gouging softer sheetrock. We kept going. It was uncomfortable and hard working above our heads with hot steam. Finally, in the midafternoon, we had all the wallpaper off. We went downstairs, grabbed a cool drink, went outside, and sat under the shade of a nearby tree. For a moment, the drink and shade were probably the best we ever enjoyed.

What was that loud crash sound coming from the open upstairs window? Did someone knock over a table with a couple of lamps on it? No, no one was in the house. We rushed upstairs. A large section of the bedroom ceiling had fallen to the floor. Pieces of plaster and plaster dust were everywhere, along with eons of attic dust and rodent-related stuff. Evidently, over the years, significant portions of the ceiling's plaster had separated from the lathe, and the multiple layers of wallpaper had been all that was holding the plaster up and together. If we had done just a little bit of due diligence from the attic side, we would have discovered this situation beforehand. Once discovered, we would have left the existing ceiling alone and moved on to simply applying sheetrock over it. Sometimes, the undoing of something is best avoided. . . . Just leave it be, don't touch it, and move on to the next step.

#21 *A little TPM goes a long way.*
DIY
A little TPM helps during DIY projects.

After two days of continuous discomfort in my left eye and two days of not being able to find anything in it or relieve the irritation, I finally went to the medical center. I knew that a piece of sawdust had flown into my eye as I power-sawed through a sheet of plywood the previous Saturday. In the past, I had always managed to extract such an irritant, or at the least, have it wash out under the running water of a hot shower. This time was different . . . no change . . . no improvement . . . no relief. So here I was at the eye clinic, missing a half day of work and feeling a little foolish as I looked around at the other patients, who seemed to have more serious eye problems. When my turn came, I explained what happened, and when the doctor looked, he didn't see sawdust resting on a hard-to-reach-recessed corner of my eye. What he saw was a splinter *stuck* in my eye! No wonder it hurt. With some magic eye drops that numbed the surface of my eyeball, he was able to pull it out quickly and easily, just like you would a splinter in your finger. For the following week, though, I had to put a special ointment in my eye and wear an eye patch that reminded me of all the pirate pictures I had ever seen. For that week, I was out of commission as far as any carpentry activity was concerned. During that time, I could also hear my father saying, as he often had when he visited and participated in a project with me, "Son, why aren't you wearing safety glasses?" "Gee, Dad, I misplaced them, and they are too scratched up to see through. I'm only going to be making a couple of quick cuts." Guess what? A week after the splinter incident, I shelved those excuses and went out and bought a quality pair of safety glasses, which now hang by the saw (easy to find and ready to use).

I must be a slow learner. The basement project was finally underway. I was going to convert an unfinished basement into a more usable family space. First things first. I drew on the floor where the new stud walls were to go. I found some dry and straight pressure-treated two-by-fours to use as the wall's floor plates. I bought a new, power-actuated nail gun for driving nails through the pressure-treated boards into the concrete floor by firing a 0.22-caliber-like bullet inside a protective chamber. It was a fun tool to use, and it worked well. One problem. I was remiss in wearing ear protection. That evening, after a couple dozen firings of that gun in the enclosed basement space, my ears were ringing. "Oh, that will go away. It's only temporary." Nope. It didn't go away and still hasn't several years later. How stupid of me.

If I had taken some simple, thoughtful, protective, and preventive measures, I could've preserved my hearing and saved myself a trip to the eye clinic. I won't make those mistakes again.

#22 Look for opportunities to develop a "better mousetrap."
➤ **DIY** ➤
I need a better way to haul lumber.

Until about age fifty, I was never fortunate to own a pickup truck, but I once owned a Buick Skylark sedan. After finishing graduate school with a diminished bank account and a growing family, that Skylark was our only vehicle. During the week, my wife shuttled me to and from work. During the weekend, I used it to bring home all my big-box-store home improvement goodies. One summer Saturday morning, flush with the excitement of a long-anticipated weekend project in my crosshairs, I headed out to buy two-by-six and two-by-eight boards for a new entrance stoop for our back door. I bought the boards and returned to my car. Hmmm, the boards were too long for the trunk, even with the back seat down. Hmmm, there were too many boards to traverse the inside of the car, from the passenger-side-front window and out the driver-side rear window. Hmmm, how do I get the boards home, twenty miles away? I was too cheap to pay for professional delivery. So, I loaded them onto the roof of the car (not the rack on the roof—there wasn't one of those). Twenty minutes later, the lumber was securely tied down left to right and front to back. With all the pent-up anticipation of a six-year-old on Christmas morning, I was ready to haul my load home with hazard lights flashing and a dutifully tacked red flag flapping in my wake. I climbed into the driver's seat and immediately felt that the inside of the car had gotten smaller. I looked up, and much to my chagrin, the roof of the car was severely bowed in. Hmmm, not good. There was no way, however, that I was going to unload that lumber any place but home. I did get the wood home, and the roof of that car was never the same. I needed a better option.

When I finally got my first pickup truck, I thought my hauling problems were over. Indeed, sheets of plywood and eight-foot-long boards were easy. Twelve-footers and longer, however, remained a challenge. Flat in the truck bed, those longer boards tenuously teetered on the tailgate. My solution was to buy a couple of forty-pound bags of gravel or mulch, whether I needed them or not, to sit on top of the cab-side ends of those longer boards. The teetering stopped. But, after a while, I had more bags of gravel and mulch at home than I'd ever need. There had to be a better way. Yes, there is. I found and bought and still use a truck bed extender that slips into the truck's trailer hitch. At the end of a long metal arm is what looks like the upper part of a football goalpost—a crossbar with two uprights. That crossbar is about three or four feet behind the truck's lowered tailgate. This reasonably priced (I would have paid double the amount) and easily installed extender is an ingenious and effective way to transport boards of almost any length and any weight. I wish I had invented and patented that device! I am very surprised the lumber stores don't sell them right next to their lumber. If you have a pickup, you could benefit from one of these. I no longer do car-roof-top hauling or needlessly add to my bags of gravel and mulch inventory. There was a simple and better way that I discovered and still use.

#23 New product ideas can emerge from anyone, anywhere, at any time.

➤ DIY ⤎

Standard products of the trade often start out as tricks of the trade.

I am convinced that there is an ex-electrician living in the lap of luxury on some exotic island, supported by the fortune they made creating a product that is nothing more than a pair of bent pliers. If you look in the tool belt of almost any electrician, you will notice what otherwise would be a normal-looking pair of needle-nosed pliers, except that the head is bent at about a thirty-degree angle to the handle. These bent pliers are indispensable when removing those large staples used to hold electric wiring in place along a rafter, joist, or wall stud. With this odd-looking pair of pliers, the procedure is a simple one: pinch the staple to be removed with the pliers' head, position the head against the flat surface of the board the staple was driven into, and then push down on the handle, forcing the head and the gripped staple to come up and out. This quick process does not damage the cable, an important point since deadly volts of electricity might be running through it. Our wealthy electrician probably had the bright idea one day to take an old pair of pliers and pound on them with a hammer to bend them just to see if they would accomplish this feat.

Lo and behold, the bent pliers did the job.

This retired electrician is sharing the island with a similarly wealthy carpenter friend. That person invented the little rubber device that attaches to the cord on an electric drill and holds the drill's chuck key (the grooved tool that is inserted into the drill's chuck and opens and closes the jaws of the chuck). One day, after misplacing the third chuck key that week, this carpenter took a piece of string or a rubber band, wrapped it around the key, and secured it to the cord. The carpenter subsequently never lost another chuck, nor have millions of other electric-drill users.

There is a third person on this luxury island. That person once had a fence building and installation company. What is a must in fence building? Getting the fence posts perfectly vertical, left to right and front to back—two simultaneous musts. Rather than continually repositioning a traditional level on two faces of a post, this person probably glued two levels together to get a ninety-degree angle between them. That then led to an epiphany to make a wraparound post level tool that simultaneously checks both dimensions—left to right and front to back—for verticality. I own one, I use it, and I wish I had invented it and patented it.

#24 *"Never too old to be wrong or too young to be right."*
⚒ DIY ⚒
Choose between old and new tools carefully.

I have and still use a radial arm saw that I bought in 1976 at a Sears store. Today, I think those types of saws are outlawed by the safety regulators, and there is probably a good reason for that. Still, over the years, I have found it to be one of the most versatile and reliable table-top saws I have seen. If it continues to give me what I need in the way of performance, no matter its age, it won't be retired anytime soon. On the other hand, I was planning a weekend of tree trimming using a chainsaw my father-in-law had used for years, and eventually, he bequeathed it to me. It had been about a year since I last used it, so I decided to take it into the shop for a tune-up. A few days later, I got the dreaded call—your chainsaw does not start, will not start, and is terminal, not economically repairable. Aging had not been kind to the chainsaw's innards. Old may be okay for some tools, but not always.

I have become a fan of the new battery-operated tools. They have enough power and accuracy to do what I often need. One such battery-powered tool that I enjoy having is a circular saw. There is no need for long extension cords. No need for ear protection. A new wood-cutting innovation not in existence when I started out as a DIYer, but a valuable tool that has been added to my workshop. On the other hand, the new metal tape measures are not nearly as long-lasting and as smoothly operating as the one I used for twenty-five years before losing it. With the new ones, it seems I must buy a replacement every couple of years. Their roll-up mechanism quits working, or the tape itself gets easily bent/kinked, or their hooking tip loosens, or the plastic locking mechanism breaks. Once a tape measure lets you down, it must go. Wish I could find a new one that would last as long as my original one. Modern versions of tools may be valuable and viable in some instances, but not always.

#25 *Simple is in.*

 DIY

Simple tools can make a huge difference.

There are two tools in my workshop that I rely on for important aspects of many projects, and yet they are probably ones that you would never name as among the most sophisticated or examples of complex engineering. For me, they are elegant and dependable in their simplicity. The first is the triangle-shaped speed square. You simply lay one leg of it against the outside edge of a board and run the edge of your circular saw against the other leg that runs along the pencil mark you made on the board to cut. It is a guaranteed method for quick, reliable, square, straight crosscuts. The second tool on my "can't do without list" is a set of pistol-grip clamps. These clamps tighten and release with one hand and yet are very strong and do not mar the wood they are clamped onto. They are invaluable when I'm doing a project by myself because they serve like an extra pair of hands. Neither of these tools required any space-age technology to make, nor do they contain any expensive components. Highly reliable, affordable, functional, durable, simple, and portable—what else could you ask for in a tool?

#26 *Fundamentals matter. Codify yours.*
DIY
Fad tools seldom do the job.

My wife has decided that I am a difficult person to buy presents for. This is not because I have everything. It is because there aren't many things that I want, and if there is something I want, I usually have already acquired it myself. Moreover, she knows that the category of gifts most likely to be appreciated is the category she knows the least about—tools. Usually, she asks me ahead of my birthday if there is a tool that I was thinking of getting but had not yet purchased.

Several years ago, however, she didn't ask. On that birthday, I picked up the last wrapped gift. It felt heavy. It was not a pair of socks. The thought occurred to me that it might be a tool, but I could not imagine what since I did not recall her asking. Sure enough, it was a tool. It was not, however, one you would find in a reputable hardware store, nor was it one you would want a pro to see in your toolbox. It was of the sort that you see advertised on the local TV station in the wee hours of the morning, where you send two payments of $19.99 to a PO box, and you get this magnificent multiuse tool, along with free shipping. This tool was a combination hammer, pliers, and wrench. No kidding! I don't recall its given name. I call it a "hapler." I am sure the TV ad made it sound like it could replace a host of tools cluttering my toolbox. After feigning some surprise and thankfulness in receiving this novel tool, I put it in my toolbox thinking, *Who knows? Maybe it will be useful for something someday.* Since that birthday, there have been a couple of instances when I gave it a try, only to learn that it is clearly inferior in all aspects to the basic tools that it was intended to replace. It is neither a good hammer, nor a good pair of pliers, nor a good wrench. Today, my "hapler" hangs on a nail in the garage, gathering dust. Frankly, I am waiting for an invitation to a birthday party for someone I am not too fond of so I can regift my "hapler."

#27 Be alert! There are at least eleven different kinds of intelligence.

🔨 DIY 🔨

There are at least five different kinds of many tools and DIY resources. It is important to know which to use for what.

Use a		
curved-claw hammer	for	general carpentry.
straight-claw hammer	for	ripping and dismantling work.
ball-peen hammer	for	metalwork.
tack hammer	for	upholstery.
sledgehammer	for	heavy pounding.

Use a		
handsaw	for	crosscutting or ripping.
backsaw	for	cabinetry joinery.
coping saw	for	small-diameter curves.
compass saw	for	large curves.
hacksaw	for	metal.
Use a		
digging shovel	for	holes and small ditches.
root-cutting shovel	for	removing bushes and trees.
edging shovel	for	flower beds.
snow shovel	for	sidewalk snow removal.
scoop shovel	for	mulch and gravel.
Use		
butt hinges	for	residential entry doors.
strap hinges	for	garden gates.
spring hinges	for	screen doors.
piano hinges	for	desk-top lids.
offset hinges	for	cabinet doors.

#28 *Be alert—again! Adults learn in particular ways.*
DIY
Trial and error. YouTube videos. Observing a pro.
Three great ways to learn.

One of the things I love about doing DIY projects is that what you just did need not be permanent if you think it can be done better. In many situations, not every aspect of how I have built a wall, finished a piece of furniture, added shelving to a room, painted trim, installed crown molding, or added beamed panels to an existing ceiling has always gone well. The beauty is being able to stop, undo what you are not pleased with, redo it in a slightly different way, and then complete the task. DIY projects often lend themselves to trial-and-error approaches that are very forgiving of mistakes or changes, foster learning, and produce better results. Jump in! You can generally redo that part of the project that you have determined is unsatisfactory with only a modest loss of time or money but replete with a worthwhile amount of learning.

YouTube offers a wealth of visual learning possibilities for DIYers. My son needed a desk. Somewhere, he had seen a beautiful wooden desk with colorful epoxy resin inlays. He wanted one like that. I was of no help on that front. He had never done something like that before either. YouTube to the rescue. By watching and rewatching a couple of videos posted there, he learned what materials to buy and how to use them. He now has a keepsake desk with a stunning top—one with a gray and turquoise epoxy stream flowing in it from top left to bottom right.

I wanted to learn how to make raised panel inset cabinet doors. I hired my trim carpenter friend for a weekend with the agreement that I could watch, help, and learn from him how to do that specific task. We did just that, and there are six beautiful cabinet doors of that type in our home. I'm not sure I could replicate what he did, but I now at least know how to try to go about it. You can learn a lot from shadowing a patient and willing expert.

#29 *Look for opportunities to lead your peers.*
➤ DIY ᐸ
Some craftsmen don't want to lead their peers.

He was an outstanding trim carpenter and cabinet maker. Customers and colleagues alike praised him for his work. He was soft-spoken and humble. The partners who founded and ran the design and build firm he worked for eventually offered him a raise and promotion to head up one of their crews. He had the "time in grade" requisite for the role. He had the well-earned collegial respect. He had the trust and confidence of the owners. The ultimate issue was that he did not have the desire to accept the offer. He did not want to be responsible for four or five others. He did not want to be involved in their job-related problems or issues or oversee their tasks and deliverables. He wanted to do his job, do it well, quietly, and without making waves. His bosses were wise. They kept him and did not put him into that leadership role. He has been with that firm now for over thirty years, still doing his own thing and doing it better than ever.

Then, there are the Todds (not a real name to protect the guilty) that I have encountered over the years. The defining trait of the Todds is that they are the child of the small firm's founder and owner. It could be a plumbing company, an HVAC company, an electrical company, or even a home-building firm. The ones I have had to deal with don't know as much about their specialty—or about management or customer service—as their owner dad or mom. The Todds did not earn the respect of this client, a client they were handed. Even though they thought they could lead and manage, they had not acquired the wisdom or experience to do so. Perhaps, they will eventually get to that point, but I know that anytime I have questions or issues, I want the founder, not the heir—not yet anyway.

#30 *Teams usually perform best under pressure or with a high calling.*
↗ DIY ↖
When excellence is needed, a deadline is looming, and the money is big, assemble the best team possible.

We were finally ready to build the pergola we talked about for years over the bluestone patio we had installed several years earlier.

Our vision was an attractive outdoor space constructed conveniently close to the house yet situated so we could enjoy the beauty and privacy of the backyard and the neighboring farm. I identified and coordinated a team committed to the same mission. After much searching, I found a kit manufacturer as the supplier of a structural fiberglass pergola that we were able to customize. I found a decorator who advised us on color. I teamed with the logistics people to get the one large, half-ton crate from the road, across my yard, avoiding the septic field, and into position next to the building site. I teamed with a concrete person to locate, level, and install the required footings. I teamed with a builder with whom I worked side by side to transform a couple hundred kit pieces into a strong and pleasing-to-the-eye pergola.

Every member of the team knew it was an expensive undertaking for me, one that was intended to enhance our lives by creating a beautiful setting for enjoying our rural property. They also knew there could be no mistakes without creating significant time delays or costly damage. Its first and impending use would be for an upcoming wedding. Excellence, cost, and deadline motivated us all to give our best and to take pride in our respective parts of the undertaking. My concrete friend and building friend were there at the end and were able to stand back with me and admire a completed job finished on time, on budget, strongly crafted, and very pleasing to the eye.

#31 *What can someone bring? The TEA$^{(squared)}$, of course.*
↗ DIY ↖
Find a building supply person with TEA$^{(squared)}$.

In general, I find the chain store home improvement outlets suitable only for common, everyday DIY items. Clerks in those stores are mostly friendly and can usually get you to the correct aisle for the store's standard stock items. The brightly vested clerks, however, are often not very helpful if you have questions about how best to configure or construct a small aspect of a DIY project. They seldom can suggest alternative materials that might be better than the basics they stock. Few, if any, know the building codes and thus are not helpful in that regard. With a few exceptions, they are mostly store clerks who could do what they do in a grocery store or a department store. That is not a criticism; the fact is that many of them are simply not knowledgeable or seasoned enough to provide DIY insights or advice beyond price and shelf location.

For many of my projects, I do not have plans that I am following. I often improvise as the project progresses. Most of the time, it all works out well because I proceed slowly and carefully. But it's nice to know I can find a friendly expert who can understand what I am trying to achieve and help me troubleshoot or even contribute new ideas, things I never would have thought of myself. I have found that just the right counter person at a locally owned building supply store can be an invaluable resource, especially once you get to know them and return to them again and again. You may pay a bit more for supplies at their store, but it has become worth it to me in several instances. Just the right counter person, who is savvy about all things building related, who is interested in DIYers and thus will take the time to explain and explore possibilities with you, is a joy. If they are someone who will also go the extra mile to make a query to one of their suppliers on your behalf or spend some time looking through their catalogs with you, they are doubly enjoyable and helpful. And, if they do all that with a pleasant attitude that does not make you feel stupid or unworthy of their attention, they are triply enjoyable. It is very worthwhile to cultivate an ongoing working relationship with a specific person at a locally owned building supply outlet who offers you their time, talent, energy, effort, and a positive attitude.

> **#32** *Empowerment requires enablement and encouragement.*
> ⚒ DIY ⚒
> *Show them and encourage them so they can then do it on their own.*

My son was fixing up an older house he and his wife had purchased. They had gotten it for a good price, it had location and potential—and it needed lots of work. One weekend, my wife and I drove down for a couple of overnights to help with their projects where we could. One of the final things my son and I began working on that weekend was re-screening his large back porch. I had done such a job years before; he never had.

The challenge in such an endeavor is to end up with an evenly stretched, not-wavey, well-secured, installed screen. We tore off the old screen, removed all the remnants of long-rusted nails and screws, and prepared a shopping list for all the needed materials. The list included galvanized staples for use in his staple gun, galvanized or stainless steel #4 common nails, pressure-treated screen door lathe strips, and a high-quality roll of screen that was the width of the top-to-bottom dimension of the porch opening to be screened. When we got back to his house, we began. He stapled one end while I held the roll. Then, as I kept mild tension on the roll, I unrolled it a bit, and he stapled it across the top and bottom of the opening as I then continued to slowly unfurl the roll. He stapled the top edge of the screen for about two or three feet before gently pulling down on that section to then staple the same two- or three-foot section across the bottom.

We arrived at a natural stopping place (lunch), cut the screen, and finished stapling what had been stretched in place. We doubled back with a few more staples and then measured and cut the lathe strips. We nailed them in place all around the perimeter of the opening as well as on any vertical two-by-four studs. The job wasn't complete, but what we had finished looked great, and I told him so. He had seen how to do it. He could finish it. My wife and I headed home. The next weekend, my son and his wife were able to finish it, and they did a great job.

#33 *Whenever possible, be more relational and less transactional.*
🔨 **DIY** 🔨
The relationship was more important than the transaction.

It was the third or fourth time I was using the same electrician for various electrical tasks at my home. Each time, I went out of my way to chat with him and get to know him just a bit better. He was affable and always seemed appreciative of my interest in his work and in him. He and two of his crew were downstairs wiring my basement one afternoon after I had spent a couple of months framing it. Off in the distance, I could hear a siren. I was in my study and noticed the siren getting closer. Someone must've been hurt nearby for an ambulance to be coming this direction. The siren got louder and closer. I went to the other side of the house and looked out the window. It was a firetruck coming down our street . . . coming up my driveway! I rushed out, and the fire department had gotten a call from my neighbor who had seen smoke coming from the lower level, the back part of my house. The neighbor had called me, but as I often do, I simply ignored the phone, so they called the volunteer fire department.

What happened? One of the electrician's helpers had gone outside to take a cigarette break. It was a windy day, and without his knowing it, some of his cigarette ashes had lodged in the nearby flower bed's dry mulch. The wind had fanned that ember into a flame after he had gone back in to resume working. The burning mulch had spewed a lot of smoke and caught a few bushes on fire, and it was that smoke my neighbor had seen.

My electrician was very apologetic, even embarrassed, and offered to pay for new mulch and new bushes. I said something akin to, no worries, we'll sort it out later. I was not angry. I was not demanding recompense. I didn't imply that his employee needed better supervision. The relationship I had established with the electrician was more important than detailing and rectifying a couple hundred dollars of damage. I never gave him a bill. He brought several bags of mulch and discounted his bill. Subsequently, he remains my go-to electrician whenever possible, and he always returns my calls.

#34 *Find and show your softer side.*
🔨 DIY 🔨
Rounded edges can soften some flaws in the construction.

For me, it has been important to learn when to pursue exactness and perfection in a weekend construction project and when it was not critical. As part of a large, two-tiered deck project at our house, there are several built-in flower boxes that stand about four feet above the lower deck level and three feet below the upper deck level. For most of the upper deck's perimeter, there is a sitting-height stub wall whose design parallels that of the flower boxes. Part of that design includes a double cap that runs the entire length of the stub wall and the flower box tops. Those caps on both structures are very visible features, and in fact, due to their height and length, this feature draws your eye, thus making it very important that it have the appearance of a perfectly straight line. After nailing in place several sixteen-foot cap boards that were not perfectly straight or had a few knot holes along their edges, I decided to remove the visual temptation to want to see a perfectly straight line. I chose to round off the long edges of those cap boards with a router. That rounding served to dampen an observer's expectation of the long-edged sight line needing to be perfectly straight. Just that simple step softened the look and made those long cap boards visually appealing.

#35 Consider making care a core strength.
 DIY
Care is often reciprocated.

Building a home long-distance is a challenge. We did that once . . . five hours driving time away. Once was enough. And to make matters even more challenging, our general contractor (GC) was two hours away from the site, and the architect/designer was seven. What were we thinking? Oh, well. Every Friday, my wife and I would drive to meet with that week's subcontractors and the GC if he could make it, which he usually couldn't (we found out later why). We quickly realized, more so than normal, that we were completely reliant on the professionalism and integrity of the subs for the successful and timely completion of the house since the GC was often absent. We would meet with that week's subs to go over that week's work, pay them, and discuss what was on the schedule for the coming week. In essence, we became the GC since ours was often AWOL.

Quite naturally, we grew to like and respect the subs (all except one that we had to fire). In turn, the subs seemed to respect what we were trying to accomplish on our own and appreciated how we dealt with them. This point came home in a kind, dramatic fashion on two occasions. Shortly after a mass campus shooting in our home state of Virginia, I got a call from my project electrician, wanting to know if I was okay and if I had been injured. As it turned out, he had my university affiliation wrong. But I appreciated his call and his concern. On a second occasion, we discovered that all our just-delivered appliances had been stolen from the jobsite. Someone had broken in through a basement door. I was lamenting this fact to my project plumber, who offered to drive by our under-construction house every evening after he got off work elsewhere in the area to make sure that day's subs had locked up and that everything seemed in order. He did that for several months. Our kindness toward him was returned multifold. Good people appreciate being cared about and are ready to reciprocate in kind ways.

#36 *Play an ACE as often as you can.*
DIY
Everyone appreciates being appreciated.

My wife is very tolerant and even appreciative (I think) of my DIY projects. She is not, however, a connoisseur of the details inherent in my carpentry and amateur engineering. This became very evident in one of my major endeavors. In converting an attic into a home theatre, I discovered that all the floor joists were spaced twenty-four inches apart. That was not a problem until I also discovered that five of those joists spanned an unsupported distance of fifteen feet. That spacing and span met the code for a storage space but not for an inhabited space. The county inspector told me something would have to be done to bring that part of the attic floor's substructure up to code. After exploring creative structural options with a building engineer, I ruled out the elaborate suggestions. In the end, the best course of action was to insert four additional, not-so-easily inserted joists in between the five that were already there. That solution created a floor joist system in that section of the attic floor with a spacing of twelve inches, which met code. After I described the problem to my wife and enticed her to the attic to see what I had done, she uttered a superlative to beat none, "It is very nice, honey, but no one will ever see it." It was clear that she was pleased that I was pleased, but she had no real comprehension—and thus no real appreciation—of the rigor with which potential solutions had been studied and discarded, the elegantly simple solution employed, or the solo-person effort involved to execute it. I love my wife for lots of reasons, none of which is her minimal DIY-appreciation quotient.

That experience highlighted my inner desire for periodic affirmation, celebration, and continued encouragement to do the seen and unseen parts of my projects well. DIY projects are often solo endeavors, so a little second-party appreciation is valued from time to time. If I had that desire, the carpenters, electricians, painters, and others that I employ from time to time must have that same inner desire to some extent. Ever since that day, I have tried to seize a moment at the end of a job to explicitly acknowledge my appreciation to those professionals for their time and talents. I love highlighting something specific in their results that I find especially well done or creatively configured. Everyone likes to be praised and appreciated!

ACKNOWLEDGMENTS

A book project is a team effort. I want to thank Miranda Dillon, Suzanne Bradshaw, the other fine folks at Koehler Books, and Amy Lemley for their professionalism, encouragement, and excellence pertaining to the manuscript and its publication. I also want to single out several Darden School colleagues for their colleagueship, collaborations, and expertise shared with me over the years—Jeanne Liedtka, Jennifer Hicks, Kathy Kane, Ed Freeman, Jim Clawson, Paul Farris, and George Shaffer—thank you! I learned a lot from each of you. I also want to acknowledge the supportive environment of the Darden School, where I have been given some wonderful opportunities to manage/lead and learn/stretch/grow.

BIO

Mark Haskins has spent most of his career as a full-time professor at the University of Virginia's internationally acclaimed Darden Graduate School of Business, known for its development of management-oriented case studies and outstanding classroom faculty. Over the years, he has taught thousands of practicing managers and future managers (MBA students). Those practicing managers have been from family-owned and stock-exchange-listed companies, governmental, and other not-for-profit agencies, they have been from around the world, and they possess many different functional specialties. He has authored (or coauthored) numerous articles appearing in a variety of management journals. He has traveled to Belgium, France, Ukraine, Brazil, Germany, Hong Kong, Switzerland, the UK, Thailand, and Australia to teach or work with managers—experiencing an enjoyable career on many dimensions! Without a doubt, however, he is most proud of his family—a son, a daughter, and seven granddaughters. He resides in the rolling hills of central Virginia with his wife of many years after having spent considerable time living in North Carolina, Colorado, California, Ohio, and Pennsylvania.

ENDNOTES

1. Tom Groneberg, *The Secret Life of Cowboys* (New York: Scribner Books, 2003), 65.

2. MQ is used here to convey a general capability for management excellence. In that regard, it is like the concept of IQ (intelligence quotient), EQ (emotional quotient), SQ (social quotient), and AQ (adversity quotient) but without a psychological instrument for assessing it.

3. See www.bls.gov/oes/current/oes110000.htm and www.bls.gov/ooh/management/# (accessed 4-25-23).

4. Grant Golliher, *Think Like a Horse* (New York: G. P. Putnam's Sons, 2022), 248.

5. John P. Kaminski, *The Quotable Jefferson* (Princeton, NJ: Princeton University Press, 2006), 201.

6. Mark Greaney, *Sierra Six* (New York: Berkley, 2022), ix. Biographical information on Choi Hong Hi, is available at https://www.itftaekwondo.com/about-us/choi-hong-hi/ (accessed 4-27-23).

7. Annie Dillard, *Pilgrim at Tinker Creek* (New York: Harper Collins, 1974), 84.

8. Mary Oliver, *Devotions: The Selected Poems of Mary Oliver* (New York: Penguin Press, 2017), 248.

9. 79.11 years = average U.S life expectancy as of 2023 per www.macrotrends.net/countries/USA/united-states/life-expectancy (accessed 5-20-23). 79.11 – 18 non adult years = 61.11 average adult years. 52 weeks per year. 168 hours per week.

10. Bob Dylan, *Love Minus Zero/No Limit*, available at https://genius.com/Bob-dylan-love-minus-zero-no-limit-lyrics

(accessed 5-19-23).

11 Sydney Finklestein, *Why Smart Executives Fail* (New York: Portfolio Books, 2003), 213-214.

12 R. Wartzman (2009), "GM: Lessons from the Alfred Sloan era," available at: https://www.bloomberg.com/news/articles/2009-06-12/gm-lessons-from-the-alfred-sloan-era (accessed 5-1-24).

13 American Public Ledger (2023), "Farewell to Circuit City: Reflections on the End of an Era," available at: https://medium.com/@americanpublicledger/farewell-to-circuit-city-reflections-on-the-end-of-an-era-6777c69c07f0 (accessed 5-31-24).

14 Stephen Ambrose, *Undaunted Courage* (New York: Simon & Schuster, 1996), 25.

15 Warren Buffett, *Warren Buffett and Business Aviation Facts* (Washington DC: National Business Aviation Association, undated), 5.

16 Paul Evans was the first person I heard posit management development programs as a means for gluing (binding) diverse and dispersed organizational units. See his article titled, "Management Development as Glue Technology," *Human Resource Planning* 15, no. 1 (1992): 85-106. My experience, as described in this vignette, bears out his proposition.

17 Pete Blaber, *The Mission, the Men, and Me* (New York: Berkley Caliber, 2008), 212.

18 Richie Norton, *The Power of Starting Something Stupid: How to crush fear, make dreams happen, and live without regret* (Salt Lake City, UT: Shadow Mountain Press, 2013), 249.

19 These teams were referred to as PICOS teams (Purchased Input Concept Optimization with Suppliers). GM had immense purchasing power and became known for exercising that power through PICOS with many of their not-so-big suppliers.

20 For more information on strategic sourcing, see Danyelle Guernsey, "Understanding the Basics: What is Strategic Sourcing?" (May 18, 2022), available at https://blog.workday.com/en-us/2022/understanding-basics-what-strategic-sourcing.html (accessed 5-11-23).

21 These two companies were noted for me as leaders in the strategic sourcing arena by my colleague, Dwai Roy.

22 Gerard O'Connell, "Pope Francis: 'Build bridges, not walls'" (March 31, 2019), available at https://www.americamagazine.org/faith/2019/03/31/pope-francis-build-bridges-not-walls (accessed 5-3-24).

23 For a target costing overview, also see S. Ansari, J. Bell, and D. Swenson, "A Template for Implementing Target Costing," *Cost Management* 20, no. 5 (2006): 20-27.

24 Mark Greaney, *One Minute Out* (New York: Berkley, 2020), 6.

25 Kevin Fedarko, *The Emerald Mile* (New York: Scribner, 2013), 21.

26 According to the dictionary (https://www.merriam-webster.com/dictionary/osmosis (accessed 5-14-23)), osmosis is the "movement of a solvent through a semi-permeable membrane into a solution of higher solute concentration that tends to equalize the concentrations of solute on the two sides of the membrane."

27 Mark Greaney, *Agent in Place* (New York: Berkley, 2018), 140.

28 Securities and Exchange Commission, *Accounting and Auditing Enforcement Release No. 1150* (August 11, 1999) available at https://www.sec.gov/litigation/admin/34-41729.htm (accessed 5-14-23).

29 "Design Defects of the Ford Pinto Gas Tank", (undated), available at https://www.fordpinto.com/archive/blowup.html (accessed 7-21-24).

30 Pete Schroeder, "Theranos and its founder settle US fraud charges: SEC," (March 14, 2018), available at https://www.reuters.com/article/us-theranos-sec-idUSKCN1GQ2HC (accessed 5-14-23).

31 Grant Golliher, *Think Like a Horse* (New York: G. P. Putnam's Sons, 2022), 24.

32 Daniel Goleman, *Focus: The Hidden Driver of Excellence* (New York: HarperCollins Publishers, 2013), 8.

33 Fred Crawford and Ryan Mathews, *The Myth of Excellence* (New York: Crown Business, 2001), xvi.

34 I first came across the notion of T-shaped skills in Pam Jones, et. al., *Delivering Exceptional Performance* (London, UK: Pitman Publishing, 1996). To this day, I still find it an appropriate way of thinking about one's own professional development agenda.

35 A bit of career advice given in a speech by Katheen K. Oberg, CFO of Marriott International, to an audience at the University of Virgnia, February 21, 2018.

36 Robert Penn Warren, *All the King's Men* (New York: Houghton Mifflin Harcourt, 1974), p. 371.

37 Todd Pierce, from Riding High Ministries newsletter (February 2020).

38 For additional questions like these, see Stephanie Vozza, "The Impact of Stay Interviews," *HR Magazine* 68, no. 1 (2023): 84-85.

39 Cormac McCarthy, *The Road* (New York: Vintage Books, 2006), 12.

40 David Baldacci, *The Whole Truth* (New York: Grand Central Publishing, 2008), 25.

41 It is worth noting that the more frequent management discussions of an 80/20 or 20/80 paradigm pertain to customer profitability analysis vis-à-vis the depiction of a "whale curve" where perhaps 20 percent of one's accounts are shown as providing 80 percent of the profits or vice versa. Such an analysis then highlights the need for possible differential customer service actions. Readers are referred to an excellent article on this "whale curve": Baker Tilly US, LLP, "Visualizing customer profitability with the whale curve," (September 8, 2020) available at https://www.bakertilly.com/insights/visualizing-customer-profitability-with-the-whale-curve (accessed 6-5-23).

42 Pete Nelson, *Treehouse Masters: The Levitating Lighthouse* (aired January 14, 2015), Animal Planet Network.

43 LIV Golf is a professional golf tour. "LIV" refers to the Roman numerals for fifty-four, the score if every hole on a par-seventy-two course were birdied and the number of holes to be played at LIV events. Source: https://en.wikipedia.org/wiki/LIV_Golf (accessed 5-8-23). In 2023, LIV and the PGA announced they would merge.

44 For an extensive example of this approach, see: M. Haskins and J. Clawson, "Seeing the Unseen: Initiating an MBA Program Committee Change Process," *International Journal of Educational Management* 20, no. 4 (2006): 304-314. The noun audit is from the Latin *auditus*, which means "a hearing, a listening." An assumptions audit aims to inquire, listen,

discuss, evaluate, and render a verdict on the assumptions operating within and across management's thinking. For the Latin root, see http://etymonline.com/search?q=audit (accessed 5-28-24).

45 Folklore typically attributes this quote to Albert Einstein. Per Quote Investigator, "Not everything that counts can be counted," (May 26, 2010) available at www.quoteinvestigator.com/2010/05/26/everything-counts-einstein/ (accessed 5-20-23), is a quote more appropriately attributed to William Bruce Cameron, *Informal Sociology* (New York: Random House, 1963), 13.

46 GAAP stands for generally accepted accounting principles and represents the measurement conventions required by the auditing profession that must review published annual reports.

47 Another great example of an organizational evolution to a revised set of performance measures is in the Major League Baseball world depicted in the movie *Moneyball* and the book on which it was based, *Moneyball: The Art of Winning an Unfair Game*, by Michael Lewis, (New York: W. W. Norton & Co., 2003).

48 Neil Postman, *Conscientious Objections* (New York: Vintage Books, 1992), 26.

49 For more information on, and ideas for asking good questions, see "10 Effective Questioning Techniques (with tips)," (September 30, 2022), available at www.indeed.com/career-advice/career-development/questioning-techniques (accessed 6-4-23).

50 Perhaps the classic example of too little probing is the woeful tale of Enron's failure. It appears that some key people did not fully understand how the company was generating its reported earnings, and in the absence of a full understanding, they seemed to simply accept the results provided to them. In the end, it all came tumbling down.

51   Nelson DeMille, *Up Country* (New York: Warner Books, 2002), 505.

52 For a more extensive discussion of this topic, readers are referred to the following two articles. R. E. Freeman and M. E. Haskins, "A Step-by-Step Process for Transforming Contentious Disagreements into Creative Collaborations," *Strategy & Leadership* 42, no. 3 (2014): 15-22. See also, S. Dmytriyev, R. E. Freeman, and M. E. Haskins, "Transforming

Disagreements into Opportunities to Enhance Learning, Decision Making, and Trust," *Strategy & Leadership* 44, no. 2 (2016): 31-38.

53 C. T. Harnsberger (ed.), *Mark Twain at your Fingertips: A book of Quotations* (Mineola, NY: Dover Publications, Inc., 2009), 180.

54 Charles A. Lindbergh, *The Spirit of St. Louis* (New York: Scribner, 2003), 352.

55 Aaron Latham, *Code of the West* (New York: Berkley Books, 2001), 25.

56 Jeanne is a long-time colleague with whom I have had many management development conversations. I have also known Chic for years and have worked with him on numerous occasions to bring his expertise to groups of managers attending some of the professional development programs I have helped design.

57 William F. Sine, *Guardian Angel* (Philadelphia, PA: Casemate, 2012), 157.

58 Jim Collins, *Good to Great* (New York: HarperBusiness, 2001), 202.

59 Consistent with the thinking presented here, see also Ed D. Hess and Jeanne M. Liedtka, "The Learning Launch: How to Grow Your Business with the Scientific Method," (June 20, 2016) available at https://ideas.darden.virginia.edu/the-learning-launch-how-to-grow-your-business-with-the-scientific-method (accessed 5-14-23).

60 Thomas Ricks, *The Generals* (New York: Penguin Books, 2012), 360.

61 A witty and wise view expressed to me by a former colleague as one her father, a Coast Guard officer, had once shared with her.

62 Kurt Vonnegut, *Hocus Pocus* (New York: Berkley Publishing Group, 1990), 238.

63 Greg Jacobson, "5 Principles of a High Reliability Organization (HRO)," (May 2023), available at https://blog.kainexus.com/improvement-disciplines/hro/5-principles (accessed 6-2-23).

64 For additional information on TPM, readers may find the following of interest: R. Mishra et. al., "A SWOT Analysis of Total Productive Maintenance Frameworks," *International*

Journal of Management Practice 3, no. 1 (2008): 51-81; Jill Jusko, "Maintenance Miscues," (April 2007): 29-32 available at www.industryweek.com, (accessed 1-4-08); also John Teresko, "Profiting from Proactive Maintenance," (August 2007): 18-20 available at www.industryweek.com, (accessed 1-4-08); and Leon Altomonte, "What is Total Productive Maintenance (TPM)? (November 2022), available at https://safetyculture.com/topics/total-productive-maintenance/ (accessed 6-2-23).

65 Quote is attributed to George Gobel at https://www.allgreatquotes.com/authors/george-gobel/ (accessed 5-22-23).

66 Marcus Luttrell, *Service* (New York: Little Brown & Co., 2012), 262.

67 Thomas Disch, *334: A Novel* (New York: Vintage Books, 1974), 25.

68 Gary Wolfe, "Steve Jobs: The Next Insanely Great Thing," Wired, (February 1, 1996), available at www.wired.com/1996/02/jobs-2/ (accessed 6-14-23).

69 See Greg Beato, "Twenty-five Years of Post-it® Notes," (March 24, 2005), available at http://www.rakemag.com/print/2506, (accessed 11-28-07).

70 Gerry House, "The Pringles® Paradigm," *Inspiring Students to Achieve* 4, no. 3 (2007): 2.

71 James Patterson and Maxine Paetro, *Private: #1 Suspect* (New York: Vision, 2012), 116.

72 Ms. Cindy Shaver, Deputy Assistant Secretary of the US Navy—Acquisition (retired), in remarks at the University of Virginia, Darden School, February 16, 2023, offering wise counsel she had received and embraced years earlier.

73 Full disclosure: My family and Eric's are friends. I have known Eric since he was in middle school, and he has always been an energetic, fun-loving, kind, smart, passionate, and creative young man. While in college, he also converted his love of playing paintball in the woods with his friends into becoming a professional paintball athlete, traveling the world. He then worked for a paintball company designing products for them.

74 Joel Cornell, "What is Quibi? Everything you need to know", (April 6, 2020), available at https://www.howtogeek.com/662501/what-is-quibi-everything-you-need-to-know/ (accessed 4-29-23). Ali Donaldson, "7 Product Launch Fails

that Defined 2022", (December 26, 2022) available at https://www.inc.com/ali-donadlson/7-product-launch-fails-that-defined-2022.html (accessed 7-22-24).

75 William Golding, *Lord of the Flies* (New York: Penguin Books, 1982), 129.

76 Mr. Immelt spoke at the University of Virginia's Darden Graduate School of Business, October 31, 2006.

77 E. Richard Brownlee II, "Wendy's Chili: A Costing Conundrum," UVA-C-2206 and UVA-C-2206TN, (Charlottesville, VA: Darden Business Publishing, 2005).

78 See www.lendingtree.com/press/executives/doug-lebda/ (accessed 4-30-23).

79 See www.lendingtree.com/content/uploads/2019/04/2019-04-17-doug-lebda-bio.pdf (4-30-23).

80 Janet Lowe, *Michael Jordan Speaks: Lessons from the World's Greatest Champion* (New York: John Wiley & Sons, 1999), back cover.

81 George S. Viereck, "What Life Means to Einstein," *Saturday Evening Post* (October 26, 1929): 117.

82 For an elaboration of all eleven intelligences, see, Charles Handy, *The Hungry Spirit* (New York: Broadway Books, 1998), 203-204.

83 Pete Blaber, *The Mission, the Men, and Me* (New York: Berkley Caliber, 2008), 113.

84 M. Knowles, E. Holton III, R. Swanson, and P. Robinson, *The Adult Learner* (New York: Routledge, 2020).

85 Stanley McChrystal, *My share of the Task: A Memoir* (New York: Portfolio/Penguin, 2013), 392.

86 Acronyms are "a word or combination of letters, taken from other words or from phrases, that is intended to aid retention." See Diane Ullius, "ART: Acronyms Reinforce Training," *Training & Development* (February 1997): 9-10.

87 Robert O'Neill, *The Operator* (New York: Scribner Books, 2017), 158.

88 Similar insights are also detailed by a colleague in his coauthored book, J. Clawson and D. Newberg, *Powered by Feel* (Singapore: World Scientific Publishing Co., 2009).

89 Erik Larson, *The Splendid and the Vile* (New York: Crown,

2020), 186.

90 Abby McCain (December 15, 2022), "25+ wasting time at work statistics (2023): How much time is wasted at work," available at https://www.zippia.com/advice/wasting-time-at-work-statistics/ (accessed 5-11-23).

91 Jim Harter, "Is Quiet Quitting Real?" (September 6, 2022) available at https://www.gallup.com/workplace/398306/quiet-quitting-real.aspx?utm_source=npr_newsletter&utm_medium=email&utm_content=20220909&utm_term=7224424&utm_campaign=money&utm_id=5861281&orgid=88&utm_att1= (accessed 5-13-23).

92 James Clawson and Mark Haskins, "Beating the Career Blues," *The Academy of Management Executive* 14, no. 3 (2000): 92.

93 Ibid., 93

94 C. T. Harnsberger ed., *Mark Twain at your Fingertips: A Book of Quotations* (Mineola, NY: Dover Publications, 2009), 354.

95 Mark Haskins and George Shaffer, "Executive Development: Planning for 'Key Experiences,'" *Development & Learning in Organizations: An International Journal* 23, no. 3 (2009): 9-13.

96 Jim Mattis and Bing West, *Call Sign Chaos* (New York: Random House, 2019), 45.

97 Pam Houston, *Cowboys are my Weakness* (New York: W.W. Norton, 1992), 144.

98 For more discussion of this topic, see Mark Haskins, Jeanne Liedtka, and John Rosenblum, "Beyond Teams: Towards an Ethic of Collaboration," *Organizational Dynamics* (Spring 1998): 36-52.

99 Ibid.

100 Charles Handy, *The Hungry Spirit* (New York: Broadway Books, 1998), 186. In my opinion, any book by Charles Handy is guaranteed to be a learning experience and a reading pleasure.

101 Pam Houston, *Deep Creek* (New York: W.W. Norton, 2019), 233.

102 Please see B. K. Cooper, J. C. Sarros, and J. C. Santora, "The Character of Leadership," *Ivey Business Journal* (2007), available at www.iveybusinessjournal.com/publication/the-character-of-leadership/ (accessed 5-12-23).

103 Galatians 5: 22-23, *The Holy Bible*.

104 Y. Tauber, "Seven Fruits of the Soul," (undated), available at www.chbad.org/library/article_cdo/aid/408049/jewish/seven-fruits-of-the-soul.htm (accessed 5-12-23).

105 Rabbi Nanus, "Musar: Spiritual practices that teach how to live a meaningful life," (May 20, 2020), available at https://resources.finalsite.net/images/v1589837378/wbtlaorg/l4j8gsbwut6esc6ytp62/MusarWorksheet.pdf (accessed 3-3-24).

106 John McCain and Mark Salter, *Why Courage Matters* (New York: Random House, 2004), 43.

107 Stephen Ambrose, *Undaunted Courage* (New York: Simon & Schuster, 1996), 74.

108 Ralph Waldo Emerson, *Everyday Emerson* (New York: St. Martin's Essentials, 2022), August 27 entry.

www.ingramcontent.com/pod-product-compliance
Lightning Source LLC
LaVergne TN
LVHW091720070526
838199LV00050B/2470